MW01001508

Seinem lieben Neffen
Ernst
von
Onkel Ernst.
Stiepel, 16.I.30

BOOKS BY
WILLIAM·J·LONG
Little Brother to the Bear
FOLLOWING THE DEER
SCHOOL OF THE WOODS
BEASTS OF THE FIELD
Northern Trails
FOWLS OF THE AIR
WAYS OF WOOD FOLK
WOOD FOLK AT SCHOOL
WILLIAM J. LONG
WILDERNESS WAYS
WILLIAM J. LONG
SECRETS OF THE WOODS
WILLIAM J. LONG

Northern
Trails

Northern Trails

Some Studies of Animal Life in the Far North

By William J. Long

Author of School of the Woods
Beasts of the Field
Fowls of the Air
Little Brother to the Bear
Following the Deer
Wood Folk Series
etc.

Illustrated by
Charles Copeland

BOSTON · U · S · A
AND LONDON
GINN & COMPANY
THE ATHENÆUM PRESS 1905

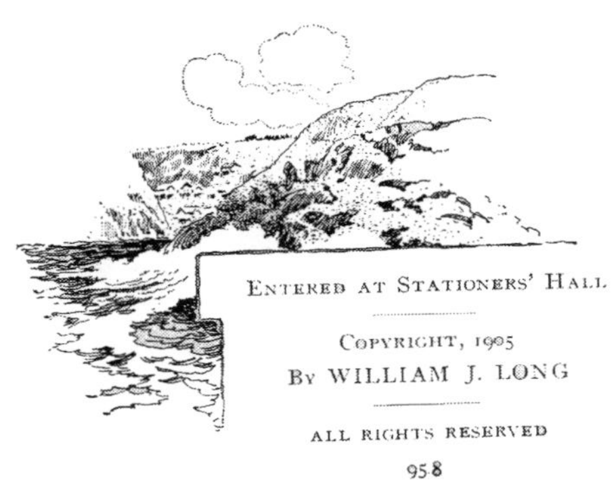

TO MY FRIEND WHO LOVES THE WILDERNESS

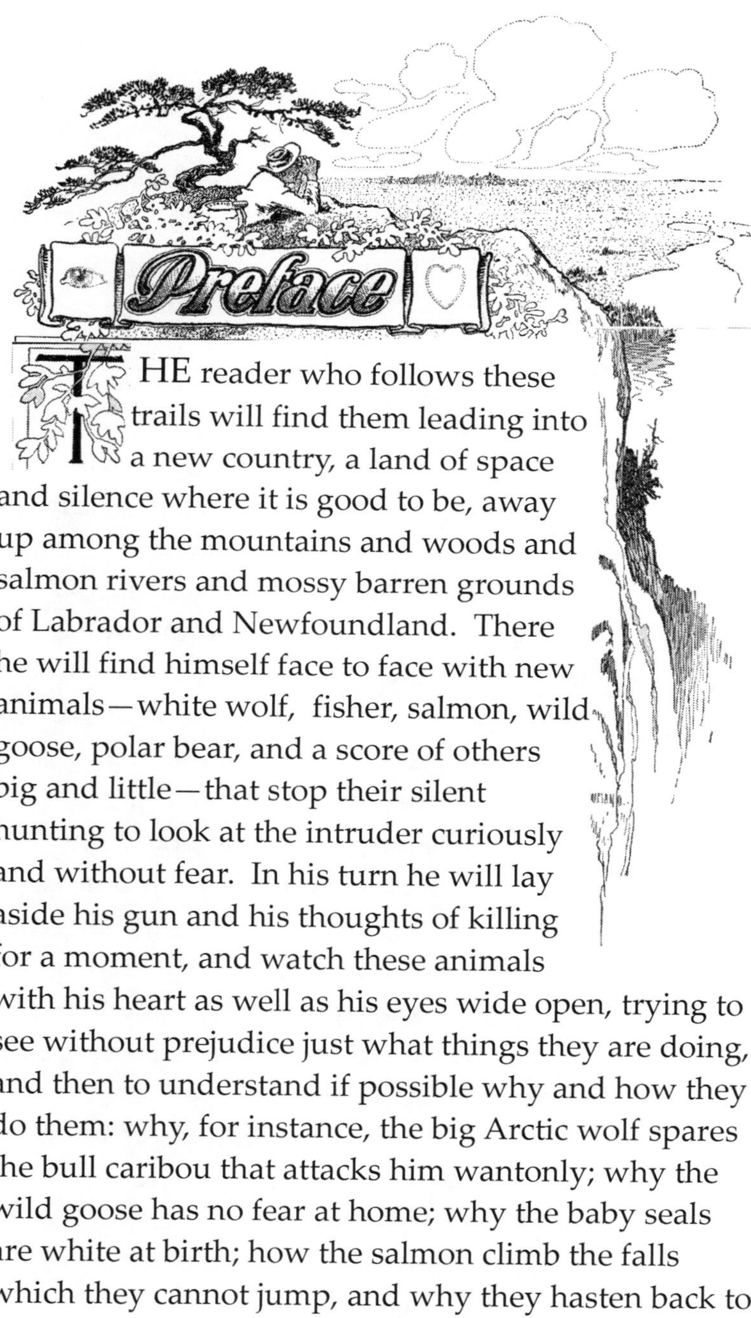

THE reader who follows these trails will find them leading into a new country, a land of space and silence where it is good to be, away up among the mountains and woods and salmon rivers and mossy barren grounds of Labrador and Newfoundland. There he will find himself face to face with new animals—white wolf, fisher, salmon, wild goose, polar bear, and a score of others big and little—that stop their silent hunting to look at the intruder curiously and without fear. In his turn he will lay aside his gun and his thoughts of killing for a moment, and watch these animals with his heart as well as his eyes wide open, trying to see without prejudice just what things they are doing, and then to understand if possible why and how they do them: why, for instance, the big Arctic wolf spares the bull caribou that attacks him wantonly; why the wild goose has no fear at home; why the baby seals are white at birth; how the salmon climb the falls which they cannot jump, and why they hasten back to

Preface

the sea when they are hurt; how the whale speaks without a voice; and what makes the fisher confuse his trail, or leave beside it a tempting bait for you when you are following him,—all these and twenty more curious things are waiting to be seen and understood at the end of the trail.

The reader who has not followed such trails before will ask at once, How many of these things are true? Every smallest incident recorded here is as true as careful and accurate observation can make it. In most of the following chapters, as in all previous volumes, will be found the direct results of my own experience among animals; and in the few cases where, as stated plainly in the text, I have used the experience of other and wiser men, I have taken the facts from first-hand and accurate observers, and have then sifted them carefully so as to retain only those that are in my own mind without a question as to their truth. In the long story of Wayeeses the White Wolf, for example,—in which for the greater interest I have put the separate facts into a more or less connected biography,—every incident in this wolf's life, from his grasshopper hunting to the cunning caribou chase, and from the den in the rocks to the meeting of wolf and children on the storm-swept barrens, is minutely true to fact, and is based squarely upon my own observation and that of my Indians.

In one case only, the story of Kopseep the Salmon, have I ventured to make an exception to this rule of absolute accuracy. For years I have followed and watched the salmon from the sea to the head-springs of his own river and back again to the sea, and all that part of his story is entirely true to fact; but beyond the breakers and beneath the tide no man has ever followed or seen him. I was obliged, therefore, either to omit that part of his life or to picture it as best I could from imagination and the records of the salmon hatcheries and deep-sea trawlers. I chose, for the story's sake, the latter course, and this part of the record has little value beyond a purely literary one. It is a guess at probable truth, and not, like the rest of the book, a record of careful observation.

If the reader find himself often wondering at the courage or gentleness or intelligence of these free folk of the wilderness, that need not trouble or puzzle him for an instant. He is not giving human traits to the beasts, but is simply finding, as all do find who watch animals closely, many things which awaken a sympathetic response in his own heart, and which he understands, more or less clearly, in precisely the same way that he understands himself and his own children.

Preface

It is not choice, but necessity, which leads us to this way of looking at animals and of trying to understand them. If we had a developed animal psychology based upon the assumption that life in one creature is essentially different from life in another, and that the intelligence in a wolf's head, for instance, is of a radically different kind from the same intelligence in the head of some other animal with two legs instead of four, then we might use our knowledge to understand what we see upon these trails. But there is no such psychology, and the assumption itself is a groundless one. Nature is of one piece, and consistent throughout. The drop is like the ocean, though it bears no ships on its bosom; the tear on a child's cheek breaks the light into glorious color, as does the rainbow on the spray of Niagara; and the law that holds the mountains fast sleeps in the heart of every grain of sand on the seashore. When we wish to measure the interstellar spaces we seek no new celestial unit, but apply confidently our own yardstick; and the chemistry that analyzes a baby's food serves equally well for the satellites of Jupiter. This is but an analogy, to be sure, but it serves to guide us in the realm of conscious life, which also seems of one piece and under one law. Inspired writers of every age have sought to comprehend even gods and angels by the same human intelligence that they applied to the ants and the conies, and for the same reason,—that they possessed but one measure of life. Love and hate, fear and courage, joy and grief, pain and pleasure, want and satisfaction,—these things, which make so large a part of life, are found in animals as well as in men, differing much in degree but not at all in kind from the same feelings in our own hearts; and we must measure them, if we are to understand them at all, by a common standard. To call a thing intelligence in one creature and reflex action in another, or to speak of the same thing as love or kindness in one and blind impulse in the other, is to be blinder ourselves than the impulse which is supposed to govern animals.

Until, therefore, we have some new chemistry that will ignore atoms and atomic law, and some new psychology that ignores animal intelligence altogether, or regards it as under a radically different law from our own, we must apply what we know of ourselves and our own motives to the smaller and weaker lives that are in some distant way akin to our own.

To cover our own blindness and lack of observation we often make a mystery and hocus-pocus of animal life by using the word *instinct* to

Preface

cover it all; as if instinct were the mysterious and exclusive possession of the animals, and not a common heritage which we share with them in large measure. It is an unmeaning word at best; for no one has told us, except in the vaguest way, what instinct is, or has set the limit where instinct ends and conscious intelligence begins, or has shown how far the primary instincts of a child differ from those of any other animal. On the other hand, one who watches animals closely and sympathetically must judge from what he sees that the motives which govern an animal's action are often very much like our own, the difference being that the animal's motive is more simple and natural than ours, and that among the higher orders the greater part of an animal's life—playing, working, seeking food, making dens, outwitting other animals, avoiding traps and enemies—is directed not by a blind instinct but by a very wide-awake intelligence. And this intelligence begins by the use of native powers and is strengthened by their daily occupation; is encouraged and developed by the mother's training and example as she leads her little ones into the world, and is perfected by the animal's own experience, which he remembers in the face of new problems—precisely as we do. A wild animal's life may indeed be far below ours, but he lives much in that pleasant borderland between thought and feeling where we so often find ourselves in our quiet moments, and there is no earthly need to make a mystery of him by talking vaguely of instinct, since so much of his life corresponds to our own and becomes intelligible to us the moment we lay aside our prejudice or hostility and watch him with a patient and friendly interest.

I make no claim whatever that animals reason or think or feel as men and women do. I have watched them too long for that; and sitting beside the beaver's village in the still twilight of the wilderness I find enough to occupy eyes and mind without making any comparison with the unquiet cities of men far away. But here before me is a life to be understood before it can be described,—a life, not an automaton, with its own joys and fears, its own problems, and its own intelligence; and the only conceivable way for me to understand it is to put myself for a moment in its place and lay upon it the measure of the only life of which I have any direct knowledge or understanding, which is my own. And this, far from being visionary or hypersensitive, as the makers of mechanical natural history would have us believe, is the only rational, indeed the only possible, way of understanding any animal action.

Preface

So, whether one looks for the facts of animal life or for the motives which govern it, the reader may follow these trails, as I first followed them, with the idea of seeing with his own eyes and understanding with his own heart. He will see many things that he does not understand, and so will listen with respect to Noel and Old Tomah, who for fifty seasons and more have lived close to the Wood Folk. And he will find at the end of every trail a real animal, as true to life as I am able to see and describe it after many years of watching in the wilderness.

WILLIAM J. LONG.
STAMFORD, CONN.,
January, 1905.

FULL PAGE ILLUSTRATIONS

WAVEESES THE STRONG ONE

Wayeeses the Strong One

The Old Wolf's Challenge

We were beating up the Straits to the Labrador when a great gale swooped down on us and drove us like a scared wild duck into a cleft in the mountains, where the breakers roared and the seals barked on the black rocks and the reefs bared their teeth on either side, like the long jaws of a wolf, to snap at us as we passed.

In our flight we had picked up a fisherman—snatched him out of his helpless punt as we luffed in a smother of spray, and dragged him aboard, like an enormous frog, at the end of the jib sheet—and it was he who now stood at the wheel of our little schooner and took her careening in through the tickle of Harbor Woe. There, in a desolate, rock-bound refuge on the Newfoundland coast, the *Wild Duck* swung to her anchor, veering nervously in the tide rip, tugging impatiently and clanking her chains as if eager to be out again in the turmoil. At sunset the gale blew itself

out, and presently the moon wheeled full and clear over the dark mountains.

Noel, my big Indian, was curled up asleep in a caribou skin by the foremast; and the crew were all below asleep, every man glad in his heart to be once more safe in a snug harbor. All about us stretched the desolate wastes of sea and mountains, over which silence and darkness brooded, as over the first great chaos. Near at hand were the black rocks, eternally wet and smoking with the fog and gale; beyond towered the icebergs, pale, cold, glittering like spires of silver in the moonlight; far away, like a vague shadow, a handful of little gray houses clung like barnacles to the base of a great bare hill whose foot was in the sea and whose head wavered among the clouds of heaven. Not a light shone, not a sound or a sign of life came from these little houses, whose shells close daily at twilight over the life within, weary with the day's work. Only the dogs were restless—those strange creatures that shelter in our houses and share our bread, yet live in another world, a dumb, silent, lonely world shut out from ours by impassable barriers.

For hours these uncanny dogs had puzzled me, a score of vicious, hungry brutes that drew the sledges in winter and that picked up a vagabond living in the idle summer by hunting rabbits and raiding the fishermen's flakes and pig-pens and by catching flounders in the sea as the tide ebbed. Venture among them with fear in your heart and they would fly at your legs and throat like wild beasts; but twirl a big stick jauntily, or better still go quietly on your way without concern, and they would skulk aside and watch you hungrily out of the corners of their surly eyes, whose lids were red and bloodshot as a mastiff's. When the moon rose I noticed them flitting about like witches on the lonely shore, miles away from the hamlet; now sitting on their tails in a solemn circle; now howling all together as if demented, and anon listening intently in the vast silence, as if they heard or smelled or perhaps just felt the presence of some unknown thing that was hidden from human senses. And when I paddled ashore to watch them one ran swiftly past without heeding me, his nose outstretched, his eyes green as foxfire in the moonlight, while the others vanished like shadows among the black rocks, each intent on his unknown quest.

That is why I had come up from my warm bunk at midnight to sit alone on the taffrail, listening

in the keen air to the howling that made me shiver, spite of myself, and watching in the vague moonlight to understand if possible what the brutes felt amid the primal silence and desolation.

A long interval of profound stillness had passed, and I could just make out the circle of dogs sitting on their tails on the open shore, when suddenly, faint and far away, an unearthly howl came rolling down the mountains, *ooooooo-ow-wow-wow*! a long wailing crescendo beginning softly, like a sound in a dream, and swelling into a roar that waked the sleeping echoes and set them jumping like startled goats from crag to crag. Instantly the huskies answered, every clog breaking out into indescribable frenzied wailings, as a collie responds in agony to certain chords of music that stir all the old wolf nature sleeping within him. For five minutes the

uproar was appalling; then it ceased abruptly and the huskies ran wildly here and there among the rocks. From far away an answer, an echo perhaps of their wailing, or, it may be, the cry of the dogs of St. Margaret's, came ululating over the deep. Then silence again, vast and unnatural, settling over the gloomy land like a winding-sheet.

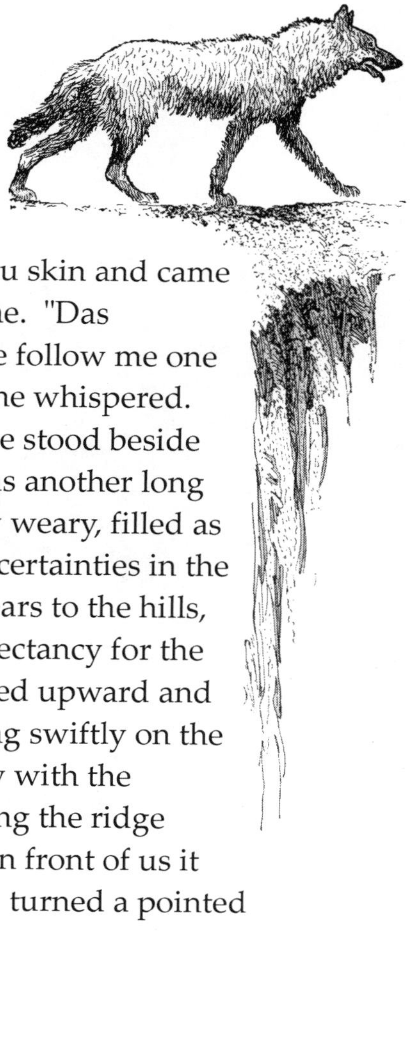

As the unknown howl trembled faintly in the air Noel, who had slept undisturbed through all the clamor of the dogs, stirred uneasily by the foremast. As it deepened and swelled into a roar that filled all the night he threw off the caribou skin and came aft to where I was watching alone. "Das Wayeeses. I know dat hwulf; he follow me one time, oh, long, long while ago," he whispered. And taking my marine glasses he stood beside me watching intently. There was another long period of waiting; our eyes grew weary, filled as they were with shadows and uncertainties in the moonlight, and we turned our ears to the hills, waiting with strained, silent expectancy for the challenge. Suddenly Noel pointed upward and my eye caught something moving swiftly on the crest of the mountain. A shadow with the slinking trot of a wolf glided along the ridge between us and the moon. Just in front of us it stopped, leaped upon a big rock, turned a pointed

"The terrible howl of the great white wolf"

nose up to the sky, sharp and clear as a fir top in the moonlight, and—*oooooo-ow-wow-wow*! the terrible howl of a great white wolf tumbled down on the husky dogs and set them howling as if possessed. No doubt now of their queer actions which had puzzled me for wolves waked to answer. Before my dull ears had heard a rumor of it they were crazy with the excitement. Now every chord in their wild hearts was twanging its thrilling answer to the leader's summons, and my own heart awoke and thrilled as it never did before to the call of a wild beast.

For an hour or more the old wolf sat there, challenging his degenerate mates in every silence, calling the tame to be wild, the bound to be free again, and listening gravely to the wailing answer of the dogs, which refused with groanings, as if dragging themselves away from overmastering temptation. Then the shadow vanished from the big rock on the mountain, the huskies fled away wildly from the shore, and only the sob of the breakers broke the stillness.

That was my first (and Noel's last) shadowy glimpse of Wayeeses, the huge white wolf which I had come a thousand miles over land and sea to study. All over the Long Range of the northern peninsula I followed him, guided sometimes by a rumor—a hunter's story or a postman's fright, caught far inland in winter and huddling close by his fire with his dogs through the long winter night—and again by a track on the shore of some lonely, unnamed pond, or the sight of a herd of caribou flying wildly from some unseen danger. Here is the white wolf's story, learned partly from much watching and following his tracks alone, but more

from Noel the Indian hunter, in endless tramps over the hills and caribou marshes and in long quiet talks in the firelight beside the salmon rivers.

Where the Trail Begins

Where the Trail Begins

FROM a cave in the rocks, on the unnamed mountains that tower over Harbor Weal on the north and east, a huge mother wolf appeared, stealthily, as all wolves come out of their dens. A pair of green eyes glowed steadily like coals deep within the dark entrance; a massive gray head rested unseen against the lichens of a gray rock; then the whole gaunt body glided like a passing cloud shadow into the June sunshine and was lost in a cleft of the rocks.

There, in the deep shadow where no eye might notice the movement, the old wolf shook off the delicious sleepiness that still lingered in all her big muscles. First she spread her slender fore paws, working the toes till they were all wide-awake, and bent her body at the shoulders till her deep chest touched the earth. Next a hind leg stretched out straight and tense as a bar, and was taken back again in nervous little jerks. At the same time she yawned mightily, wrinkling her nose and showing her red gums with the black fringes and the long white fangs that could reach a deer's heart in a single snap. Then she leaped upon a great rock and sat up straight, with her bushy tail curled close about her fore paws, a savage, powerful, noble-looking beast, peering down gravely over the green mountains to the shining sea.

A moment before the hillside had appeared utterly lifeless, so still and rugged and desolate that one must notice and welcome the stir of a mouse or ground squirrel in the moss, speaking of life that is glad and free and vigorous even in the deepest solitudes; yet now, so quietly did the old wolf appear, so perfectly did her rough gray coat blend with the rough gray rocks, that the hillside seemed just as tenantless as before. A stray wind seemed to move the mosses, that was all. Only where the mountains once slept now they seemed wide-awake. Keen eyes saw every moving thing, from the bees in the bluebells to the slow fishing-boats far out at sea; sharp ears that were cocked like a collie's heard every chirp and trill and rustle, and a nose that understood everything was holding up every vagrant breeze and searching it for its message. For the cubs were coming out for the first time to play in the big world, and no wild mother ever lets that happen without first taking infinite precautions that her little ones be not molested nor made afraid.

A faint breeze from the west strayed over the mountains and instantly the old wolf turned her sensitive nose to question it. There on her right, and just across a deep ravine where a torrent went leaping down to the sea in hundred-foot jumps, a great stag caribou was standing, still as a stone, on a lofty pinnacle, looking down over the marvelous panorama spread wide beneath his feet. Every day Megaleep came there to look, and the old wolf in her daily hunts often crossed the deep path which he had worn through the moss from the wide table-lands over the ridge to this sightly place where he could look down curiously at the comings and goings of men on the sea. But at this season when small game was abundant—and indeed at all seasons when not hunger-driven—the wolf was peaceable and the caribou were not molested. Indeed the big stag knew well where the old wolf denned. Every east wind brought her message to his nostrils; but secure in his own strength and in the general peace which prevails in the summer-time among all large animals of the north, he came daily to look down on the harbor and wag his ears at the fishing-boats, which he could never understand.

Strange neighbors these, the grim, savage mother wolf of the mountains, hiding her young in dens of the rocks, and the wary, magnificent wanderer of the broad caribou barrens; but they understood each other, and neither wolf nor caribou had any fear or hostile intent one for the other. And this is not strange at all, as might be supposed by those who think animals are governed by fear on one hand and savage cruelty on the other, but is one of the commonest things to be found by those who follow faithfully the northern trails.

Wayeeses had chosen her den well, on the edge of the untrodden solitudes—sixty miles as the crow flies—that stretch northward from Harbor Weal to Harbor Woe. It was just under the ridge, in a sunny hollow among the rocks, on the southern slope of the great mountains. The earliest sunshine found the place and warmed it, bringing forth the bluebells for a carpet, while in every dark hollow the snow lingered all summer long, making dazzling white patches on the mountain; and under the high waterfalls, that looked from the harbor like bits of silver ribbon stretched over the green woods, the ice clung to the rocks in fantastic knobs and gargoyles, making cold, deep pools for the trout to play in. So it was both cool and warm there, and whatever the weather the gaunt old mother wolf could always find just the right spot to sleep away the afternoon. Best of all it was perfectly safe; for though from the door of her den she could look down on the old Indian's cabin, like a pebble on the shore, so steep were the billowing hills and so impassable the ravines that no human foot ever trod the place, not even in autumn when the fishermen left their boats at anchor in Harbor Weal and camped inland on the paths of the big caribou herds.

Whether or not the father wolf ever knew where his cubs were hidden only he himself could tell. He was an enormous brute, powerful and cunning beyond measure, that haunted the lonely thickets and ponds bordering the great caribou barrens over the ridge, and that kept a silent watch, within howling distance, over the den which he never saw. Sometimes the mother wolf met him on her wanderings and they hunted together. Often he brought the game he had caught, a fox or a young goose; and sometimes when she had hunted in vain he met her, as if he had understood her need from a distance, and led her to where he had buried two or three of the rabbits that swarmed in the thickets. But spite of the attention and the indifferent watch which he kept, he never ventured near the den, which he could have found easily enough by following the mother's track. The old she-wolf would have flown at his throat like a fury had he showed his head over the top of the ridge.

The reason for this was simple enough to the savage old mother, though there are some things about it that men do not yet understand. Wolves, like cats and foxes, and indeed like most wild male animals, have an atrocious way of killing their own young when they find them unprotected; so the mother animal searches out a den by herself and rarely allows the male to come near it. Spite of this beastly habit it must be said honestly of the old he-wolf that he shows a marvelous gentleness towards his mate. He runs at the slightest show of teeth from a mother wolf half his size, and will stand meekly a snap of the jaws or a cruel gash of the terrible fangs in his flank without defending himself. Even our hounds seem to have inherited something of this primitive wolf trait, for there are seasons when, unless urged on by men, they will not trouble a mother wolf or fox. Many times, in the early spring, when foxes are mating, and again later when they are heavy with young and incapable of a hard run, I have caught my hounds trotting meekly after a mother fox, sniffing her trail indifferently and sitting down with heads turned aside when she stops for a moment to watch and yap at them disdainfully. And when you call them they come shamefaced; though in winter-time, when running the same fox to death, they pay no more heed to your call than to the crows clamoring over them. But we must return to Wayeeses, sitting over her den on a great gray rock, trying every breeze, searching every movement, harking to every chirp and rustle before bringing her cubs out into the world.

Satisfied at last with her silent investigation she turned her head towards the den. There was no sound, only one of those silent, unknown communications that pass between animals. Instantly there was a scratching, scurrying, whining, and three cubs tumbled out of the dark hole in the rocks, with fuzzy yellow fur and bright eyes and sharp ears and noses, like collies, all blinking and wondering and suddenly silent at the big bright world which they had never seen before, so different from the dark den under the rocks.

Indeed it was a marvelous world that the little cubs looked upon when they came out to blink and wonder in the June sunshine. Contrasts everywhere, that made the world seem too big for one little glance to comprehend it all. Here the sunlight streamed and danced and quivered on the warm rocks; there deep purple cloud shadows rested for hours, as if asleep, or swept over the mountain side in an endless game of fox-and-geese with the sunbeams. Here the birds trilled, the bees hummed in the bluebells, the brook roared and sang on its way to the sea; while over all the harmony of the world brooded a silence too great to be disturbed. Sunlight and shadow, snow and ice, gloomy ravines and dazzling mountain tops, mayflowers and singing birds and rustling winds filled all the earth with color and movement and melody. From under their very feet great masses of rock, tossed and tumbled as by a giant's play, stretched downwards to where the green woods began and rolled in vast billows to the harbor, which shone and sparkled in the sun, yet seemed no bigger than their mother's paw. Fishing-boats with shining sails hovered over it, like dragon-flies, going and coming from the little houses that sheltered together under the opposite mountain, like a cluster of gray toadstools by a towering pine stump. Most wonderful, most interesting of all was the little gray hut on the shore, almost under their feet, where little Noel and the Indian children played with the tide like fiddler crabs, or pushed bravely out to meet the fishermen in a bobbing nutshell. For wolf cubs are like collies in this, that they seem to have a natural interest, perhaps a natural kinship with man, and next to their own kind nothing arouses their interest like a group of children playing.

So the little cubs took their first glimpse of the big world, of mountains and sea and sunshine, and children playing on the shore, and the world was altogether too wonderful for little heads to comprehend. Nevertheless one plain impression remained, the same that you see in the ears and nose and stumbling feet and wagging tail of every puppy-dog you meet on the streets, that this bright world is a famous place, just made a-purpose for little ones to play in. Sitting on their tails in a solemn row the wolf cubs bent their heads and pointed their noses gravely at the sea. There it was, all silver and blue and boundless, with tiny white sails dancing over it, winking and flashing like entangled bits of sunshine; and since the eyes of a cub, like those of a little child, cannot judge distances, one stretched a paw at the nearest sail, miles away, to turn it over and make it go the other way. They turned up their heads sidewise and blinked at the sky, all blue and calm and infinite, with white clouds sailing over it like swans on a limpid lake; and one stood up on his hind legs and reached up both paws, like a kitten, to pull down a cloud to play with. Then the wind stirred a feather near them, the white feather of a ptarmigan which they had eaten yesterday, and forgetting the big world and the sail and the cloud, the cubs took to playing with the feather, chasing and worrying and tumbling over each other, while the gaunt old mother wolf looked down from her rock and watched and was satisfied.

NOEL AND MOOKA

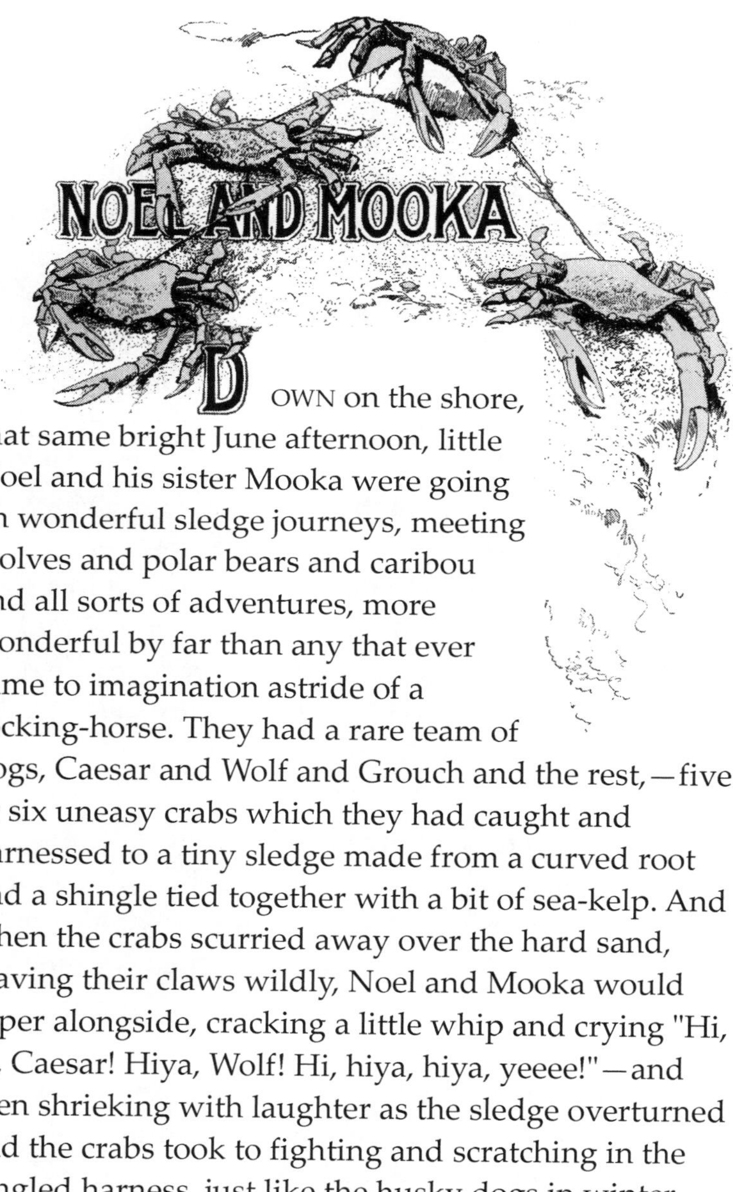

NOEL AND MOOKA

DOWN on the shore, that same bright June afternoon, little Noel and his sister Mooka were going on wonderful sledge journeys, meeting wolves and polar bears and caribou and all sorts of adventures, more wonderful by far than any that ever came to imagination astride of a rocking-horse. They had a rare team of dogs, Caesar and Wolf and Grouch and the rest,—five or six uneasy crabs which they had caught and harnessed to a tiny sledge made from a curved root and a shingle tied together with a bit of sea-kelp. And when the crabs scurried away over the hard sand, waving their claws wildly, Noel and Mooka would caper alongside, cracking a little whip and crying "Hi, hi, Caesar! Hiya, Wolf! Hi, hiya, hiya, yeeee!"—and then shrieking with laughter as the sledge overturned and the crabs took to fighting and scratching in the tangled harness, just like the husky dogs in winter. Mooka was trying to untangle them, dancing about to keep her bare toes and fingers away from the nipping claws, when she jumped up with a yell, the biggest crab hanging to the end of her finger.

"Owee! oweeeee! Caesar bit me," she wailed. Then she stopped, with finger in her mouth, while Caesar scrambled headlong into the tide; for Noel was standing on the beach pointing at a brown sail far down in the deep bay, where Southeast Brook came singing from the green wilderness.

"Ohé, Mooka! there's father and Old Tomah come back from salmon fishing."

"Let's go meet um, little brother," said Mooka, her black eyes dancing; and in a wink crabs and sledges were forgotten. The old punt was off in a shake, the tattered sail up, skipper Noel lounging in the stern, like an old salt, with the steering oar, while the crew, forgetting her nipped finger, tugged valiantly at the main-sheet.

They were scooting away gloriously, rising and pounding the waves, when Mooka, who did not have to steer and whose restless glance was roving over every bay and hillside, jumped up, her eyes round as lynx's.

"Look, Noel, look! There's Megaleep again watching us." And Noel, following her finger, saw far up on the mountain a stag caribou, small and fine and clear as a cameo against the blue sky, where they had so often noticed him with wonder watching them as they came shouting home with the tide. Instantly Noel threw himself against the steering oar; the punt came up floundering and shaking in the wind.

"Come on, little sister; we can go up Fox Brook. Tomah showed me trail." And forgetting the salmon, as they had a moment before forgotten the crabs and sledges, these two children of the wild, following every breeze and bird call and blossoming bluebell and shining star alike, tumbled ashore and went hurrying up the brook, splashing through the shallows, darting like kingfishers over the points, and jumping like wild goats from rock to rock. In an hour they were far up the mountain, lying side by side on a great flat rock, looking across a deep impassable valley and over two rounded hilltops, where the scrub spruces looked like pins on a cushion, to the bare, rugged hillside where Megaleep stood out like a watchman against the blue sky.

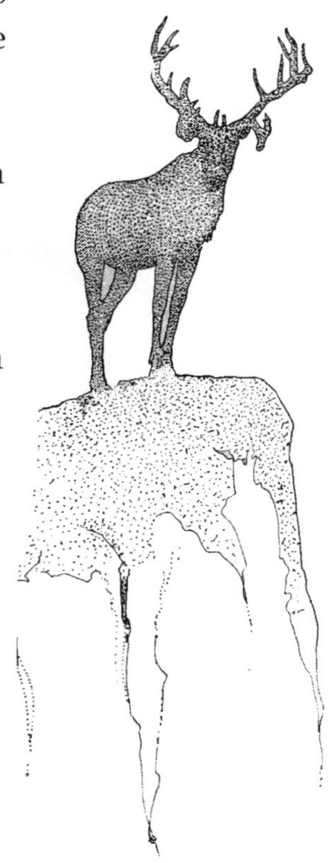

"Does he see us, little brother?" whispered Mooka, quivering with excitement and panting from the rapid climb.

"See us? sartin, little sister;

Noel and Mooka

but that only make him want peek um some more," said the little hunter. And raised carelessly on his elbows he was telling Mooka how Megaleep the caribou trusted only his nose, and how he watched and played peekaboo with anything which he could not smell, and how in a snowstorm—

Noel was off now like a brook, babbling a deal of caribou lore which he had learned from Old Tomah the hunter, when Mooka, whose restless black eyes were always wandering, seized his arm.

"Hush, brother, and look, oh, look! there on the big rock!"

Noel's eyes had already caught the Indian trick of seeing only what they look for, and so of separating an animal instantly from his surroundings, however well he hides. That is why the whole hillside seemed suddenly to vanish, spruces and harebells, snow-fields and drifting white clouds all grouping themselves, like the unnoticed frame of a picture, around a great gray rock with a huge shaggy she-wolf keeping watch over it, silent, alert, motionless.

Something stirred in the shadow of the old wolf's watch-tower, tossing and eddying and growing suddenly quiet, as if the wind were playing among dead oak leaves. The keen young eyes saw it instantly, dilating with surprise and excitement. The next instant they had clutched each other's arms.

"Ooooo!" from Mooka.

"Cubs; keep still!" from Noel.

And shrinking close to the rock under a friendly dwarf spruce they lay still as two rabbits, watching with round eyes, eager but unafraid, the antics of three brown wolf cubs that were chasing the flies and tumbling over some invisible plaything before the door of the den.

Hardly had they made the discovery when the old wolf

slipped down from the rock and stood for an instant over her little ones. Why the play should stop now, while the breeze was still their comrade and the sunshine was brighter than ever, or why they should steal away into the dark den more silently than they had come, none of the cubs could tell. They felt the order and they obeyed instantly—and that is always the wonder of watching little wild things at play. The old mother wolf vanished among the rocks and appeared again higher on the ridge, turning her head uneasily to try every breeze and rustle and moving shadow. Then she went questing into the spruce woods, feeling but not understanding some subtle excitement in the air that was not there before, and only the two Indian children were left keeping watch over the great wild hillside.

For over an hour they lay there expectantly, but nothing stirred near the den; then they too slipped away, silently as the little wild things, and made their slow way down the brook, hand in hand in the deepening shadows. Scarcely had they gone when the bushes stirred and the old she-wolf, that had been ranging every ridge and valley since she disappeared at the unknown alarm, glided over the spot where a moment before Mooka and Noel had been watching. Swiftly, silently she followed their steps; found the old trails coming up and the fresh trails returning; then, sure at last that no danger threatened her own little ones, she loped away up the hill and over the topmost ridge to the caribou barrens and the thickets where young rabbits were already stirring about in the twilight.

That night, in the cabin under the cliffs, Old Tomah had to rehearse again all the wolf lore learned in sixty years of hunting: how, fortunately for the deer, these enormous wolves had never been abundant and were now very rare, a few having been shot, and more poisoned in the starving times, and the rest having vanished, mysteriously as wolves do, for some unknown reason. Bears, which are easily trapped and shot and whose skins are worth each a month's wages to the fishermen, still hold their own and even increase on the great island; while the wolves, once more numerous, are slowly vanishing, though they are never hunted, and not even Old Tomah himself could set a trap cunningly enough to catch one. The old hunter told, while Mooka and Noel held their breaths and drew closer to the light, how once, when he made his camp alone under a cliff on the lake shore, seven huge wolves, white as the snow, came racing swift and silent over the ice straight at the fire which he had barely time to kindle; how he shot two, and the others, seizing the fish he had just caught through the ice for his own supper, vanished over the bank; and he could not say even now whether they meant him harm or no. Again, as he talked and the grim old face lighted up at the memory, they saw him crouched with his sledge-dogs by a blazing fire all the long winter night, and around him in the darkness blazing points of light, the eyes of wolves flashing back the firelight, and gaunt white forms flitting about like shadows, drawing nearer and nearer with ever-growing boldness till they seized his largest dog —though the brute lay so near the fire that his hair singed—and whisked it away with an appalling outcry. And still again, when Tomah was lost three days in the interior, they saw him wandering with his pack over endless barrens and through gloomy spruce woods, and near him all the time a young wolf that followed his steps quietly, with half-friendly interest, and came no nearer day or night.

All these things and many more the children heard from Old Tomah, and among all his hunting experiences and the stories and legends which he told them there was not one to make them afraid. For the horrible story of Red Riding Hood is not known among the Indians, who know well how untrue the tale is to wolf nature, and how foolish it is to frighten children with false stories of wolves and bears, misrepresenting them as savage and bloodthirsty brutes, when in truth they are but shy, peace-loving animals, whose only motive toward man, except when crazed by wounds or hunger, is one of childish curiosity. All these ferocious animal stories have their origin in other centuries and in distant lands, where they may possibly have been true, but more probably are just as false to animal nature; for they seem to reflect not the shy animal that men glimpsed in the woods, but rather the boastings of some hunter, who always magnifies his own praise by increasing the ferocity of the game he has killed, or else the pure imagination of some ancient nurse who tried to increase her scant authority by frightening her children with terrible tales. Here certainly the Indian attitude of kinship, gained by long centuries of living near to the animals and watching them closely, comes nearer to the truth of things. That is why little Mooka and Noel could listen for hours to Old Tomah's animal stories and then go away to bed and happy dreams, longing for the light so that they might be off again to watch at the wolf's den.

One thing only disturbed them for a moment. Even these children had wolf memories and vied with Old Tomah in eagerness of telling. They remembered one fearful winter, years ago, when most of the families of the little fishing village on the East Harbor had moved far inland to sheltered cabins in the deep woods to escape the cold and the fearful blizzards of the coast. One still moonlit night, when the snow lay deep and the cold was intense and all the trees were cracking like pistols in the frost, a mournful howling rose all around their little cabin. Light footfalls sounded on the crust; there were scratchings at the very door and hoarse breathings at every crack; while the dogs, with hackles up straight and stiff on their necks, fled howling under beds and tables. And when Mooka and Noel went fearfully with their mother to the little window—for the men were far away on a caribou hunt—there were gaunt white wolves, five or six of them, flitting restlessly about in the moonlight, scratching at the cracks and even raising themselves on their hind legs to look in at the little windows.

Mooka shivered a bit when she remembered the uncanny scene, and felt again the strong pressure of her mother's arms holding her close; but Old Tomah brushed away her fears with a smile and a word, as he had always done when, as little children, they had showed fear at the thunder or the gale or

the cry of a wild beast in the night, till they had grown to look upon all Nature's phenomena as hiding a smile as kindly as that of Old Tomah himself, who had a face wrinkled and terribly grim, to be sure, but who could smile and tell a story so that every child trusted him. The wolves were hungry, starving hungry, he said, and wanted only a dog, or one of the pigs. And Mooka remembered with a bright laugh the two unruly pigs that had been taken inland as a hostage to famine, and that must be carefully guarded from the teeth of hungry prowlers, for they would soon be needed to keep the children themselves from starving. Every night at early sunset, when the trees began to groan and the keen winds from the mountains came whispering through the woods, the two pigs were taken into the snug kitchen, where with the dogs they slept so close to the stove that she could always smell pork a-frying. Not a husky dog there but would have killed and eaten one of these little pigs if he could have caught him around the corner of the house after nightfall, though you would never have suspected it if you had seen them so close together, keeping each other warm after the fire went out. And besides the dogs and the wolves there were lynxes—big, round-headed, savage-looking creatures—that came prowling out of the deep woods every night, hungry for a taste of the little pigs; and now and

then an enormous polar bear, that had landed from an iceberg, would shuffle swiftly and fearlessly among the handful of little cabins, leaving his great footprints in every yard and tearing to pieces, as if made of straw, the heavy log pens to which some of the fishermen had foolishly confided their pigs or sheep. He even entered the woodsheds and rummaged about after a stray fishbone or an old sealskin boot, making a great rowdydow in the still night; and only the smell of man, or the report of an old gun fired at him by some brave woman out of the half-open window, kept him from pushing his enormous weight against the very doors of the cabins.

Thinking of all these things, Mooka forgot her fears of the white wolves, remembering with a kind of sympathy how hungry all these shy prowlers must be to leave their own haunts, whence the rabbits and seals had vanished, and venture boldly into the yards of men. As for Noel, he remembered with regret that he was too small at the time to use the long bow which he now carried on his rabbit and goose hunts; and as he took it from the wall, thrumming its chord of caribou sinew and fingering the sharp edge of a long arrow, he was hoping for just such another winter, longing to try his skill and strength on some of these midnight prowlers—a lynx, perhaps, not to begin too largely on a polar bear. So there was no fear at all, but only an eager wonder, when they followed up the brook next day to watch at the wolf's den. And even when Noel found a track, a light oval track, larger but more slender than a dog's, in some moist sand close beside their own footprints and evidently following them, they remembered only the young wolf that had followed Tomah and pressed on the more eagerly.

Day after day they returned to their watch-tower on the flat rock, under the dwarf spruce at the head of the brook, and lying there side by side they watched the play of the young wolf cubs. Every day they grew more interested as the spirit of play entered into themselves, understanding the gladness of the wild rough-and-tumble when one of the cubs lay in wait for another and leaped upon him from ambush; understanding also something of the feeling of the gaunt old she-wolf as she looked down gravely from her gray rock watching her growing youngsters. Once they brought an old spyglass which they had borrowed from a fisherman, and through its sea-dimmed lenses they made out that one of the cubs was larger than the other two, with a droop at the tip of his right ear, like a pointed leaf that has been creased sharply between the fingers. Mooka claimed that wolf instantly for her own, as if they were watching the husky puppies, and by his broken ear said she should know him again when he grew to be a big wolf, if he should ever follow her, as his father perhaps had followed Old Tomah; but Noel, thinking of his bow and his long arrow with the sharp point, thought of the winter night long ago and hoped that his two wolves would know enough to keep away when the pack came again, for he did not see any way to recognize and spare them, especially in the moonlight. So they lay there making plans and dreaming dreams, gentle or savage, for the little cubs that played with the feathers and grasshoppers and cloud shadows, all unconscious that any eyes but their mother's saw or cared for their wild, free playing.

Something bothered the old she-wolf in these days of watching. The den was still secure, for no human foot had crossed the deep ravine or ventured nearer than the opposite hilltop. Her nose told her that unmistakably; but still she was uneasy, and whenever the cubs were playing she felt, without knowing why, that she was being watched. When she trailed over all the ridges in the twilight, seeking to know if enemies had been near, she found always the scent of two human beings on a flat rock under the dwarf spruces; and there were always the two trails coming up and going down the brook. She followed once close behind the two children, seeing them plainly all the way, till they came in sight of the little cabin under the cliff, and from the door her enemy man came out to meet them. For these two little ones, whose trail she knew, the old she-wolf, like most mother animals in the presence of children, felt no fear nor enmity whatever. But they watched her den and her own little ones, that was sure enough; and why should any one watch a den except to enter some time and destroy? That is a question which no mother wolf could ever answer; for the wild animals, unlike

"Watching her growing youngsters"

dogs and blue jays and men, mind strictly their own business and pay no attention to other animals. They hate also to be watched; for the thought of watching always suggests to their minds that which follows,—the hunt, the rush, the wild break-away, and the run

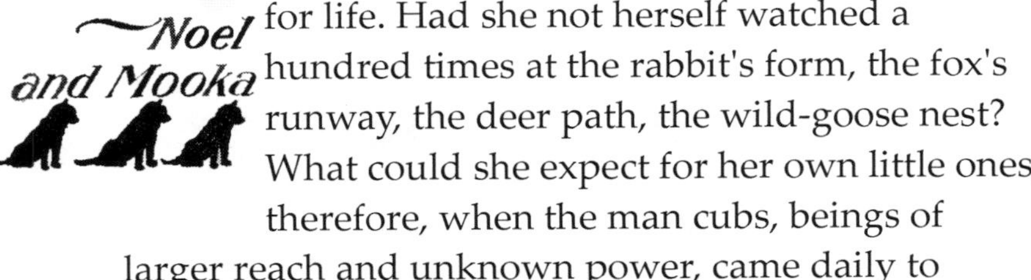

for life. Had she not herself watched a hundred times at the rabbit's form, the fox's runway, the deer path, the wild-goose nest? What could she expect for her own little ones, therefore, when the man cubs, beings of larger reach and unknown power, came daily to watch at her den?

All this unanswered puzzle must have passed through the old wolf's head as she trotted up the brook away from the Indian cabin in the twilight. When in doubt trust your fears,—that is wolf wisdom in a nutshell; and that marks the difference between a wolf and a caribou, for instance, which in doubt trusts his nose or his curiosity. So the old wolf took counsel of her fears for her little ones, and that night carried them one by one in her mouth, as a cat carries her kittens, miles away over rocks and ravines and spruce thickets, to another den where no human eye ever looked upon their play.

"Shall we see them again, little brother?" said Mooka wistfully, when they had climbed to their watch-tower for the third time and seen nothing. And Noel made confident answer:

"Oh, yes, we see um again, lil sister. Wayeeses got um wandering foot; go 'way off long ways; bimeby come back on same trail. He jus' like Injun, like um old camp best. Oh, yes, sartin we see um again." But Noel's eyes looked far away as he spoke, and in his heart he was thinking of his bow and his long arrow with the sharp point, and of a moonlit night with white shapes flitting noiselessly over the snow and scratching at the door of the little cabin.

THE WAY
OF THE
WOLF

The Way of the Wolf

A NEW experience had come to the little wolf cubs in a single night,—the experience of fear. For weeks they had lain hid in the dark den, or played fearlessly in the bright sunshine, guarded and kept at every moment, day or night, by the gaunt old mother wolf that was their only law, their only companion. At times they lay for hours hungry and restless, longing to go out into the bright world, yet obeying a stronger will than their own, even at a distance. For, once a wild mother in her own dumb way has bidden her little ones lie still, they rarely stir from the spot, refusing even to be dragged away from the nest or den, knowing well the punishment in store if she return and find them absent. Moreover, it is useless to dissimulate, to go out and play and then to be sleeping innocently with the cubs when the old wolf's shadow darkens the entrance. No concealment is possible from wolf's nose; before she enters the den the mother knows perfectly all that has happened since she went away. So the days glided by peacefully between sleep and play, the cubs trusting absolutely in the strength and tenderness that watched over them, the mother building the cubs' future on the foundation of the two instincts which are strong in every wild creature born into a world of danger,—the instinct to lie still and let nature's coloring hide all defenseless little ones, and the instinct to obey instantly a stronger will than their own.

There was no fear as yet, only instinctive wariness; for fear comes largely from others' example, from alarms and excitement and cries of danger, which only the grown animals understand. The old wolf had been undisturbed; no dog or hunter had chased her; no trap or pitfall had entangled her swift feet. Moreover, she had chosen her den well, where no man had ever stood, and where only the eyes of two children had seen her at a distance. So the little ones grew and played in the sunshine, and had yet to learn what fear meant.

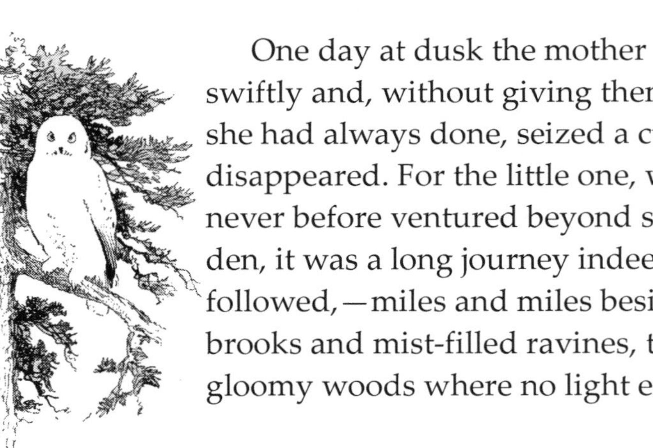

One day at dusk the mother entered swiftly and, without giving them food as she had always done, seized a cub and disappeared. For the little one, which had never before ventured beyond sight of the den, it was a long journey indeed that followed,—miles and miles beside roaring brooks and mist-filled ravines, through gloomy woods where no light entered, and over bare ridges where the big stars sparkled just over his ears as he hung, limp as a rabbit skin, from his mother's great jaws. An owl hooted dismally, *whoo-hooo!* and though he knew the sound well in his peaceful nights, it brought now a certain shiver. The wind went sniffing suspiciously among the spruce branches; a startled bird chirped and whirred away out of their path; the brook roared among the rocks; a big salmon jumped and tumbled back with resounding splash, and jumped again as if the otter were after him. There was a sudden sharp cry, the first and last voice of a hare when the weasel rises up in front of him; then silence, and the fitful rustle of his mother's pads moving steadily, swiftly over dry leaves. And all these sounds of the wilderness night spoke to the little cub of some new thing, of swift feet that follow and of something unknown and terrible that waits for all unwary wild things. So fear was born.

The long journey ended at last before a dark hole in the hillside; and the smell of his mother, the only familiar thing in his first strange pilgrimage, greeted the cub from the rocks on either side as he passed in out of the starlight. He was dropped without a sound in a larger den, on some fresh-gathered leaves and dead grass, and lay there all alone, very

still, with the new feeling trembling all over him. A long hour passed; a second cub was laid beside him, and the mother vanished as before; another hour, and the wolf cubs were all together again with the mother feeding them. Nor did any of them know where they were, nor why they had come, nor the long, long way that led back to where the trail began.

Next day when they were called out to play they saw a different and more gloomy landscape, a chaos of granite rocks, a forest of evergreen, the white plunge and rolling mist of a mountain torrent; but no silver sea with fishing-boats drifting over it, like clouds in the sea over their heads, and no gray hut with children running about like ants on the distant shore. And as they played they began for the first time to imitate the old mother keeping guard over them, sitting up often to watch and listen and sift the winds, trying to understand what fear was, and why they had been taken away from the sunny hillside where the world was so much bigger and brighter than here. But home is where mother is,—that, fortunately, is also true of the little Wood Folk, who understand it in their own savage way for a season,—and in their wonder at their new surroundings the memory of the old home gradually faded away. They never knew with what endless care the new den had been chosen; how the mother, in the days when she knew she was watched, had searched it out and watched over it and put her nose to every ridge and ravine and brook-side, day after day, till she was sure that no foot save that of the wild things had touched the soil within miles of the place. They felt only a greater wildness, a deeper solitude; and they never forgot, though they were unmolested, the strange feeling that was born in them on that first terrifying night journey in their mother's jaws.

Soon the food that was brought home at dawn —the rabbit or grouse, or the bunch of rats hanging by their tails, with which the mother supplemented their midday drink of milk—became altogether too scant to satisfy their clamorous appetites; and in the bright afternoons and the long summer twilights the mother led them forth on short journeys to hunt for themselves. No big caribou or cunning fox cub, as one might suppose, but "rats and mice and such small deer" were the limit of the mother's ambition for her little ones. They began on stupid grubs that one could find asleep under stones and roots, and then on beetles that scrambled away briskly at the first alarm, and then, when the sunshine was brightest, on grasshoppers,—lively, wary fellows that zipped and buzzed away just when you were sure you had them, and that generally landed from an astounding jump facing in a different direction, like a flea, so as to be ready for your next move.

It was astonishing how quickly the cubs learned that game is not to be picked up tamely, like huckleberries, and changed their style of hunting,—creeping, instead of trotting openly so that even a porcupine must notice them, hiding behind rocks and bushes and tufts of grass till the precise moment came, and then leaping with the swoop of a goshawk on a ptarmigan. A wolf that cannot catch a grasshopper has no business hunting rabbits—this seemed to be the unconscious motive that led the old mother, every sunny afternoon, to ignore the thickets where game was hiding plentifully and take her cubs to the dry, sunny plains on the edge of the caribou barrens. There for hours at a time they hunted elusive grasshoppers, rushing helter-skelter over the dry moss, leaping up to strike at the flying game with their paws like a kitten, or snapping wildly to catch it in their mouths and coming down with a back-breaking wriggle to keep themselves from tumbling over on their heads. Then on again, with a droll expression and noses sharpened like exclamation points, to find another grasshopper.

Small business indeed and often ludicrous, this playing at grasshopper hunting. So it seems to us; so also, perhaps, to the wise old mother, which knew all the ways of game, from crickets to caribou and from ground sparrows to wild geese. But play is the first great educator,—that is as true of animals as of men,—and to the cubs their rough helter-skelter after hoppers was as exciting as a stag hunt to the pack, as full of surprises as the wild chase through the soft snow after a litter of lynx kittens. And though they knew it not, they were learning things every hour of the sunny, playful afternoons that they would remember and find useful all the days of their life.

So the funny little hunt went on, the mother watching gravely under a bush where she was inconspicuous, and the cubs, full of zest and inexperience, missing the flying tidbits more often than they swallowed them, until they learned at last to locate all game accurately before chasing or alarming it; and that is the rule, learned from hunting grasshoppers, which a wolf follows ever afterward. Even after they knew just where the grasshopper was hiding, watching them after a jump, and leaped upon him swiftly from a distance, he often got away when they lifted their paws to eat him. For the grasshopper was not dead under the light paw, as they supposed, but only pressed into the moss waiting for his chance to jump. Then the cubs learned another lesson: to hold their game down with both paws pressed closely together, inserting their noses like a wedge and keeping every crack of escape shut tight until they had the slippery morsel safe under their back teeth. And even then it was deliciously funny to watch their expression as they chewed, opening their jaws wide as if swallowing a rabbit, snapping them shut again as the grasshopper wiggled; and always with a doubt in their close-set eyes, a questioning twist of head and ears, as if they were not quite sure whether or not they were really eating him.

Another suggestive thing came out in these hunts, which you must notice whether you watch wolves or coyotes or a den of fox cubs. Though no sound came from the watchful old mother, the cubs seemed at every instant under absolute control. One would rush away pell-mell after a hopper, miss him and tumble away again, till he was some distance from the busy group on the edge of the big lonely barren. In the midst of his chase the mother would raise her head and watch the cub intently. No sound was uttered that human ears could hear; but the chase ended right there, on the instant, and the cub came trotting back like a well-broken setter at the whistle. It was marvelous beyond comprehension, this absolute authority and this silent command that brought a wolf back instantly from the wildest chase, and that kept the cubs all together under the watchful eyes that followed every movement. No wonder wolves are intelligent in avoiding every trap and in hunting together to outwit some fleet-footed quarry with unbelievable cunning. Here on the edge of the vast, untrodden barren, far from human eyes, in an ordinary family of wolf cubs playing wild and free, eager, headstrong, hungry, yet always under control and instantly subject to a wiser head and a stronger will than their own, was the explanation of it all. Later, in the bitter, hungry winter, when a big caribou was afoot and the pack hot on his trail, the cubs would remember the lesson, and every free wolf would curb his hunger, obeying the silent signal to ease the game and follow slowly while the leader raced unseen through the woods to head the game and lie in ambush by the distant runway.

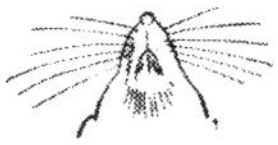

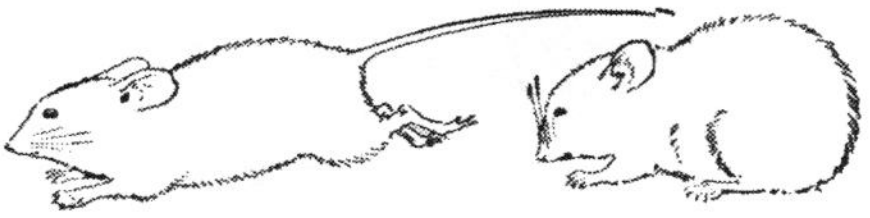

From grasshoppers the cubs took to hunting the wood-mice that nested in the dry moss and swarmed on the edges of every thicket. This was keener hunting; for the wood-mouse moves like a ray of light, and always makes at least one false start to mislead any that may be watching for him. The cubs soon learned that when Tookhees appeared and dodged back again, as if frightened, it was not because he had seen them, but just because he always appears that way. So they crouched and hid, like a cat, and when a gray streak shot over the gray moss and vanished in a tuft of grass they leaped for the spot—and always found it vacant. For Tookhees always doubles on his trail, or burrows for a distance under the moss, and never hides where he disappears. It took the cubs a long while to find that out; and then they would creep and watch and listen till they could locate the game by a stir under the moss, and pounce upon it and nose it out from between their paws, just as they had done with the grasshoppers. And when they crunched it at last like a ripe plum under their teeth it was a delicious tidbit, worth all the trouble they had taken to get it. For your wolf, unlike the ferocious, grandmother-eating creature of the nursery, is at heart a peaceable fellow, most at home and most happy when mouse hunting.

There was another kind of this mouse chasing which furnished better sport and more juicy mouthfuls to the young cubs. Here and there on the Newfoundland mountains the snow lingers all summer long. In every northern hollow of the hills you see, from a distance, white patches no bigger than your hat sparkling in the sun; but when you climb there, after bear or caribou, you find great snow-fields, acres in extent and from ten to a hundred feet deep, packed close and hard with the pressure of a thousand winters. Often when it rains in the valleys, and raises the salmon rivers to meet your expectations, a thin covering of new snow covers these white fields; and then, if you go there, you will find the new page written all over with the feet of birds and beasts. The mice especially love these snow-fields for some unknown reason. All along the edges you find the delicate, lacelike tracery which shows where little feet have gone on busy errands or played together in the moonlight; and if you watch there awhile you will surely see Tookhees come out of the moss and scamper across a bit of snow and dive back to cover under the moss again, as if he enjoyed the feeling of the cold snow under his feet in the summer sunshine. He has tunnels there, too, going down to solid ice, where he hides things to keep which would spoil if left in the heat of his den under the mossy stone, and when food is scarce he draws upon these cold-storage rooms; but most of his summer snow journeys, if one may judge from watching him and from following his tracks, are taken for play or comfort, just as the bull caribou comes up to lie in the snow, with the strong sea wind in his face, to escape the flies which swarm in the thickets below. Owl and hawk, fox and weasel and wildcat,—all the prowlers of the day and night have long since discovered these good hunting-grounds and leave the prints of wing and claw over the records of the wood-mice; but still Tookhees returns, led by his love of the snow-fields, and thrives and multiplies spite of all his enemies.

One moonlit night the old wolf took her cubs to the edge of one of these snow-fields, where the eager eyes soon noticed dark streaks shooting hither and yon over the bare white surface. At first they chased them wildly; but one might as well try to catch a moonbeam, which has not so many places to hide as a wood-mouse. Then, remembering the grasshoppers, they crouched and crept and so caught a few. Meanwhile old mother wolf lay still in hiding, contenting herself with snapping up the game that came to her, instead of chasing it wildly all over the snow-field. The example was not lost; for imitation is strong among intelligent animals, and most of what they learn is due simply to following the mother. Soon the cubs were still, one lying here under shadow of a bush, another there by a gray rock that lifted its head out of the snow. As a dark streak moved nervously by one of these hiding-places there would be a rush, a snap, the *pchap pchap* of jaws crunching a delicious morsel; then all quiet again, with only gray, innocent-looking shadows resting softly on the snow. So they moved gradually along the edges of the great white field; and next morning the tracks were all there, plain as daylight, telling their silent story of good hunting.

To vary their diet the mother now took them down to the shore to hunt among the rocks for ducks' eggs. They were there by the hundreds, scattered along the lonely bays just above high-water line, where the eiders had their nests.

At first old mother wolf showed them where to look, and when she had found a clutch of eggs would divide them fairly, keeping the hungry cubs in order

at a little distance and bringing each one his share, which he ate without interference. Then when they understood the thing they scattered nimbly to hunt for themselves, and the real fun began.

Now a cub, poking his nose industriously into every cranny and under every thick bush, would find a great roll of down plucked from the mother bird's breast, and scraping the top off carefully with his paw, would find five or six large pale-green eggs, which he gobbled down, shells, ducklings and all, before another cub should smell the good find and caper up to share it. Again he would be startled out of his wits as a large brown bird whirred and fluttered away from under his very nose. Sitting on his tail he would watch her with comical regret and longing till she tumbled into the tide and drifted swiftly away out of danger; then, remembering what he came for, he would turn and follow her trail back to the nest out of which she had stolen at his

approach, and find the eggs all warm for his breakfast. And when he had eaten all he wanted he would take an egg in his mouth and run about uneasily here and there, like a dog with a bone when he thinks he is watched, till he had made a sad crisscross of his trail and found a spot where none could see him. There he would dig a hole and bury his egg and go back for more; and on his way would meet another cub running about with an egg in his mouth, looking for a spot where no one would notice him.

From mice and eggs the young cubs turned to rabbits and hares; and these were their staple food ever afterward when other game was scarce and the wood-mice were hidden deep under the winter snows, safe at last for a little season from all their enemies. Here for the first time the father wolf appeared, coming in quietly one late afternoon, as if he knew, as he probably did, just when he was needed. Beyond a glance he paid no attention whatever to the cubs, only taking his place opposite the mother as the wolves started abreast in a long line to beat the thicket.

By night the cubs had already caught several rabbits, snapping them up as they played heedlessly in the moonlight, just as they had done with the wood-mice. By day, however, the hunting was entirely different. Then the hares and rabbits are resting in their hidden forms under the ferns, or in a hollow between the roots of a brown stump. Like game birds, whether on the nest or sitting quiet in hiding, the rabbits give out far less scent at such times than when they are active; and the cubs, stealing through the dense cover like shadows in imitation of the old wolves, and always hunting upwind, would use their keen noses to locate Moktaques before alarming him. If a cub succeeded, and snapped up a rabbit before the surprised creature had time to gather headway, he dropped behind with his catch, while the rest went slowly, carefully, on through the cover. If he failed, as was generally the case at first, a curious bit of wolf intelligence and wolf training came out at once.

As the wolves advanced the father and mother would steal gradually ahead at either end of the line, rarely hunting themselves, but drawing the nearest cub's attention to any game they had discovered, and then moving silently to one side and a little ahead to watch the result. When the cub rushed and missed, and the startled rabbit went flying away, whirling to left or right as rabbits always do, there would be a lightning change at the end of the line. A terrific rush, a snap of the long jaws like a steel trap,—then the old wolf would toss back the rabbit with a broken back, for the cub to finish him. Not till the cubs first, and then the mother, had satisfied their hunger would the old he-wolf hunt for himself. Then he would disappear, and they would not see him for days at a time, until food was scarce and they needed him once more.

One day, when the cubs were hungry and food scarce because of their persistent hunting near the den, the mother brought them to the edge of a dense thicket where rabbits were plentiful enough, but where the cover was so thick that they could not follow the frightened game for an instant. The old he-wolf had appeared at a distance and then vanished; and the cubs, trotting along behind the mother, knew nothing of what was coming or what was expected of them. They lay in hiding on the lee side of the thicket, each one crouching under a bush or root, with the mother off at one side perfectly hidden as usual.

Presently a rabbit appeared, hopping along in a crazy way, and ran plump into the jaws of a wolf cub, which leaped up as if out of the ground, and pulled down his game from the very top of the high jump which Moktaques always gives when he is suddenly startled. Another and another rabbit appeared mysteriously, and doubled back into the cover before they could be caught. The cubs were filled with wonder. Such hunting was never seen before; for rabbits stirred

abroad by day, and ran right into the hungry mouths instead of running away. Then, slinking along like a shadow and stopping to look back and sniff the wind, appeared a big red fox that had been sleeping away the afternoon on top of a stump in the center of the thicket.

The old mother's eyes began to blaze as Eleemos drew near. There was a rush, swift and sudden as the swoop of an eagle; a sharp call to follow as the mother's long jaws closed over the small of the back, just as the fox turned to leap away. Then she flung the paralyzed animal back like a flash; the young wolves tumbled in upon him; and before he knew what had happened Eleemos the Sly One was stretched out straight, with one cub at his tail and another at his throat, tugging and worrying and grumbling deep in their chests as the lust of their first fighting swept over them. Then in vague, vanishing glimpses the old he-wolf appeared, quartering swiftly, silently, back and forth through the thicket, driving every living thing down-wind to where the cubs and the mother were waiting to receive it.

That one lesson was enough for the cubs, though years would pass before they could learn all the fine points of this beating the bush: to know almost at a glance where the game, whether grouse or hare or fox or lucivee, was hiding in the cover, and then for one wolf to drive it, slowly or swiftly as the case might require, while the other hid beside the

"As the mother's long jaws closed over the small of the back"

most likely path of escape. A family of grouse must be coaxed along and never see what is driving them, else they will flit into a tree and be lost; while a cat must be startled out of her wits by a swift rush, and sent flying away before she can make up her stupid mind what the row is all about. A fox, almost as cunning as Wayeeses himself, must be made to think that some dog enemy is slowly puzzling out his cold trail; while a musquash searching for bake-apples, or a beaver going inland to cut wood for his winter supplies of bark, must not be driven, but be followed up swiftly by the path or canal by which he has ventured away from the friendly water.

All these and many more things must be learned slowly at the expense of many failures, especially when the cubs took to hunting alone and the old wolves were not there to show them how; but they never forgot the principle taught in that first rabbit drive,—that two hunters are better than one to outwit any game when they hunt intelligently together. That is why you so often find wolves going in pairs; and when you study them or follow their tracks you discover that they play continually into each other's hands. They seem to share the spoil as intelligently as they catch it, the wolf that lies beside the runway and pulls down the game giving up a portion gladly to the companion that beats the bush, and rarely indeed is there any trace of quarreling between them.

Like the eagles—which have long since learned the advantage of hunting in pairs and of scouting for game in single file—the wolves, when hunting deer on the open barrens where it is difficult to conceal their advance, always travel in files, one following close behind the other; so that, seen from in front where the game is watching, two or three wolves will appear like a lone animal trotting across the plain. That alarms the game far less at first; and not until the deer starts away does the second wolf appear, shooting out from behind the leader. The sight of another wolf appearing suddenly on his flank throws a young deer into a panic, in which he is apt to lose his head and be caught by the cunning hunters.

Curiously enough, the plains Indians, who travel in the same way when hunting or scouting for enemies, first learned the trick—so an old chief told me, and it is one of the traditions of his people—from watching the timber wolves in their stealthy advance over the open places.

The wolves were stealing through the woods all together, one late summer afternoon, having beaten a cover without taking anything, when the puzzled cubs suddenly found themselves alone. A moment before they had been trotting along with the old wolves, nosing every cranny and knot hole for mice and grubs, and stopping often for a roll and frolic, as young cubs do in the gladness of life; now they pressed close together, looking, listening, while a subtle excitement filled all the woods. For the old wolves had disappeared, shooting ahead in great, silent bounds, while the cubs waited with ears cocked and noses quivering, as if a silent command had been understood.

The silence was intense; not a sound, not a stir in the quiet woods, which seemed to be listening with the cubs and to be filled with the same thrilling expectation. Suddenly the silence was broken by heavy plunges far ahead, *crash! bump! bump!* and there broke forth such an uproar of yaps and howls as the cubs had never heard before. Instantly they broke away on the trail, joining their shrill yelpings to the clamor, so different from the ordinary stealthy wolf hunt, and filled with a nameless excitement which they did not at all understand till the reek of caribou poured into their hungry nostrils; whereupon they yelped louder than ever. But they did not begin to understand the matter till they caught glimpses of gray backs bounding hither and yon in the underbrush, while the two great wolves raced easily on either side, yapping sharply to increase the excitement, and guiding the startled, foolish deer as surely, as intelligently, as a pair of collies herd a flock of frightened sheep.

When the cubs broke out of the dense cover at last they found the two old wolves sitting quietly on their tails before a rugged wall of rocks that stretched away on either hand at the base of a great bare hill. In front of them was a young cow caribou, threatening savagely with horns and hoofs, while behind her cowered two half-grown fawns crowded into a crevice of the rocks. Anger, rather than fear, blazed out in the mother's mild eyes. Now she turned swiftly to press her excited young ones back against the sheltering wall; now she whirled with a savage grunt and charged headlong at the wolves, which merely leaped aside and sat down silently again to watch the game, till the cubs raced out and hovered uneasily about with a thousand questions in every eye and ear and twitching nostril.

The reason for the hunt was now plain enough. Up to this time the caribou had been let severely alone, though they were very numerous, scattered through the dense coverts in every valley and on every hillside. For Wayeeses is no wanton killer, as he is so often represented to be, but sticks to small game whenever he

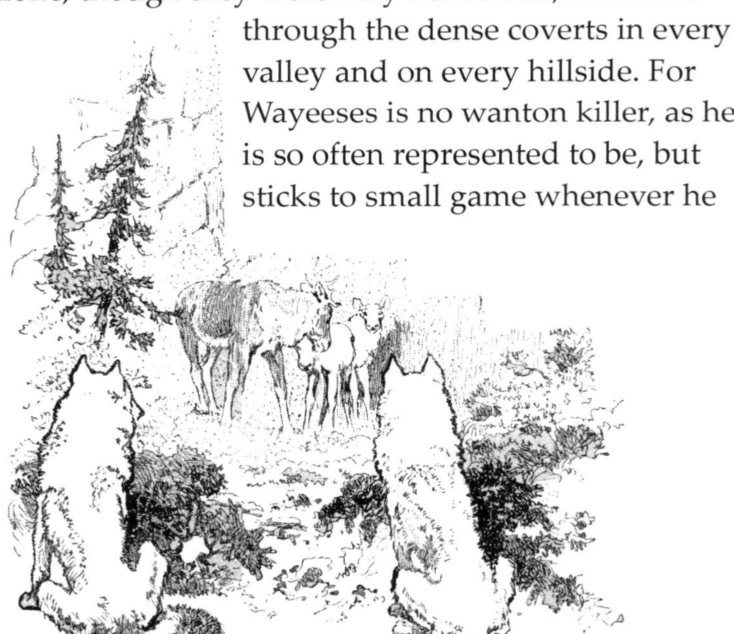

can find it, and leaves the deer unmolested. As for his motive in the matter, who shall say, since no one understands the half of what a wolf does every day? Perhaps it is a mere matter of taste, a preference for the smaller and more juicy tidbits; more likely it is a combination of instinct and judgment, with a possible outlook for the future unusual with beasts of prey. The moment the young wolves take to harrying the deer—as they invariably do if the mother wolf be not with them—the caribou leave the country. The herds become, moreover, so wild and suspicious after a very little wolf hunting that they are exceedingly difficult of approach; and there is no living thing on earth, not even a white wolf or a trained greyhound, that can tire or overtake a startled caribou. The swinging rack of these big white wanderers looks easy enough when you see it; but when the fleet staghounds are slipped, as has been more than once tested in Newfoundland, try as hard as they will they cannot keep within sight of the deer for a single quarter-mile, and no limit has ever yet been found, either by dog or wolf, to Megaleep's tirelessness. So the old wolves, relying possibly upon past experience, keep the cubs and hold themselves strictly to small game as long as it can possibly be found. Then when the bitter days of late winter come, with their scarcity of small game and their unbearable hunger, the wolves turn to the caribou as a last resort, killing a few here by stealth, rather than speed, and then, when the game grows wild, going far off to another range where the deer have not been disturbed and so can be approached more easily.

On this afternoon, however, the old mother wolf had run plump upon the caribou and her fawns in the midst of a thicket, and had leaped forward promptly to round them up for her hungry cubs. It would have been the easiest matter in the world for an old wolf to hamstring one of the slow fawns, or the mother caribou herself as she hovered in the rear to defend her young; but there were other thoughts in the shaggy gray head that had seen so much hunting. So the mother wolf drove the deer slowly, puzzling them more and more, as a collie distracts the herd by his yapping, out into the open where her cubs might join in the hunting.

The wolves now drew back, all save the mother, which advanced hesitatingly to where the caribou stood with lowered head, watching every move. Suddenly the cow charged, so swiftly, furiously, that the old wolf seemed almost caught, and

tumbled away with the broad hoofs striking savagely at her flanks. Farther and farther the caribou drove her enemy, roused now to frenzy at the wolf's nearness and apparent cowardice. Then she whirled in a panic and rushed back to her little ones, only to find that all the other wolves, as if frightened by her furious charge, had drawn farther back from the cranny in the rocks.

Again the old she-wolf approached cautiously, and again the caribou plunged at her and followed her lame retreat with headlong fury. An electric shock seemed suddenly to touch the huge he-wolf. Like a flash he leaped in on the fawns. One quick snap of the long jaws with the terrible fangs; then, as if the whole thing were a bit of play, he loped away easily with the cubs, circling to join the mother wolf, which strangely enough did not return to the attack as the caribou charged back, driving the cubs and the old he-wolf away like a flock of sheep. The coast was now clear, not an enemy in the way; and the mother caribou, with a triumphant bleat to her fawns to follow, plunged back into the woods whence she had come.

One fawn only followed her. The other took a step or two, sank to his knees, and rolled over on his side. When the wolves drew near quietly, without a trace of the ferocity or the howling clamor with which such scenes are usually pictured, the game was quite dead, one quick snap of the old wolf's teeth just behind the fore legs having pierced the heart more surely than a hunter's bullet. And the mother caribou, plunging wildly away through the brush with the startled fawn jumping at her heels, could not know that her mad flight was needless; that the terrible enemy which had spared her and let her go free had no need nor desire to follow.

The fat autumn had now come with its abundant fare, and the caribou were not again molested. Flocks of grouse and ptarmigan came out of the thick coverts, in which they had been hiding all summer, and began to pluck the berries of the open plains, where they could easily be waylaid and caught by the growing wolf cubs. Plover came in hordes, sweeping over the Straits from the Labrador; and when the wolves surrounded a flock of the queer birds and hitched nearer and nearer, sinking their gray bodies in the yielding gray moss till they looked like weather-worn logs, the hunting was full of tense excitement, though the juicy mouthfuls were few and far between. Fox cubs roamed abroad away from their mothers, self-willed and reveling in the abundance; and it was now easy for two of the young wolves to drive a fox out of his daytime cover and catch him as he stole away.

After the plover came the ducks in myriads, filling the ponds and flashets of the vast barrens with tumultuous quacking; and the young wolves learned, like the foxes, to decoy the silly birds by rousing their curiosity. They would hide in the grass, while one played and rolled about on the open shore, till the ducks saw him and began to stretch their necks and gabble their amazement at the strange thing, which they had never seen before. Shy and wild as he naturally is, a duck, like a caribou or a turkey, must take a peek at every new thing. Now silent, now gabbling all together, the flock would veer and scatter and draw together again, and finally swing in toward the shore, every neck drawn straight as a string the better to see what was going on. Nearer and nearer they would come, till a swift rush out of the grass sent them off headlong, splashing and quacking with crazy clamor. But one or two always stayed behind with the wolves to pay the price of curiosity.

Then there were the young geese, which gathered in immense flocks in the shallow bays, preparing

and drilling for the autumn flight. Late in the afternoon the old mother wolf with her cubs would steal down through the woods, hiding and watching the flocks, and following them stealthily as they moved along the shore. At night the great flock would approach a sandbar, well out of the way of rocks and brush and everything that might hide an enemy, and go to sleep in close little family groups on the open shore. As the night darkened four shadows would lengthen out from the nearest bank of shadows, creeping onward to the sand-bar with the slow patience of the hours. A rush, a startled *honk!* a terrific clamor of wings and throats and smitten water. Then the four shadows would rise up from the sand and trot back to the woods, each with a burden on its shoulders and a sparkle in the close-set eyes over the pointed jaws, which were closed on the neck of a goose, holding it tight lest any outcry escape to tell the startled flock what had happened.

Besides this abundant game there were other good things to eat, and the cubs rarely dined of the same dish twice in succession. Salmon and big sea-trout swarmed now in every shallow of the clear brooks, and, after spawning, these fish were much weakened and could easily be caught by a little cunning. Every day and night the tide ebbed and flowed, and every tide left its contribution in windrows of dead herring and caplin, with scattered crabs and mussels for a relish, like plums in a pudding. A wolf had only to trot for a mile or two along the tide line of a lonely beach, picking up the good things which the sea had brought him, and then go back to sleep or play satisfied. And if Wayeeses wanted game to try his mettle and cunning, there were the big fat seals barking on the black rocks, and he had only to cut between them and the sea and throw himself upon the largest seal as the herd floundered ponderously back to safety. A wolf rarely grips and holds an enemy; he snaps and lets go, and snaps again at every swift chance; but here he must either hold fast or lose his big game; and what between holding and letting go, as the seals whirled with bared teeth and snapped viciously in turn, as they scrambled away to the sea, the wolves had a lively time of it. Often indeed, spite of three or four wolves, a big seal would tumble into the tide, where the sharks followed his bloody trail and soon finished him.

Now for the first time the wolves, led by the rich abundance, began to kill more than they needed for food and to hide it away, like the squirrels, in anticipation of the coming winter. Like the blue and the Arctic foxes, a strange instinct to store things seems to stir dimly at times within them. Occasionally, instead of eating and sleeping after a kill, the cubs, led by the mother wolf, would hunt half of the day and night and carry all they caught to the snow-fields. There each one would search out a cranny in the rocks and hide his game, covering it over deeply with snow to kill the scent of it from the prowling foxes. Then for days at a time they would forget the coming winter, and play as heedlessly as if the woods would always be as full of game as now; and again the mood would be upon them strongly, and they would kill all they could find and hide it in another place. But the instinct—if indeed it were instinct, and not the natural result of the mother's own experience—was weak at best; and the first time the cubs were hungry or lazy they would trail off to the hidden store. Long before the spring with its bitter need was upon them they had eaten everything, and had returned to the empty storehouse at least a dozen times, as a dog goes again and again to the place where he once hid a bone, and nosed it all over regretfully to be quite sure that they had overlooked nothing.

More interesting to the wolves in these glad days than the game or the storehouse, or the piles of caplin which they cached under the sand on the shore, were the wandering herds of caribou,—splendid old stags with massive antlers, and long-legged, inquisitive fawns trotting after the sleek cows, whose heads carried small pointed horns, more deadly by far than the stags' cumbersome antlers. Wherever the wolves went they crossed the trails of these wanderers swarming out of the thickets, sometimes by twos and threes, and again in straggling, endless lines converging upon the vast open barrens where the caribou gathered to select their mates for another year. Where they all came from was a mystery that filled the cubs' heads with constant wonder. During the summer you see little of them,—here a cow with her fawn hiding deep in the cover, there a big stag standing out like a watchman on the mountain top; but when the early autumn comes they are everywhere, crossing rivers and lakes at regular points, and following deep paths which their ancestors have followed for countless generations.

The cows and fawns seemed gentle and harmless enough, though their very numbers filled the young wolves with a certain awe. After their first lesson it would have been easy enough for the cubs to have killed all they wanted and to grow fat and lazy as the bears, which were now stuffing themselves before going off to sleep for the winter; but the old mother wolf held them firmly in check, for with plenty of small game everywhere, all wolves are minded to go quietly about their own business and let the caribou follow their own ways. When October came it brought the big stags into the open,—splendid, imposing beasts, with swollen necks and fierce red eyes and long white manes tossing in the wind. Then the wolves had to stand aside; for the stags roamed over all the land, pawing the moss in fury, bellowing their hoarse challenge, and charging like a whirlwind upon every living thing that crossed their paths.

When the mother wolf, with her cubs at heel, saw one of these big furies at a distance she would circle prudently to avoid him. Again, as the cubs hunted rabbits, they would hear a crash of brush and a furious challenge as some quarrelsome stag winded them; and the mother with her cubs gathered close about her would watch alertly for his headlong rush. As he charged out the wolves would scatter and leap nimbly aside, then sit down on their tails in a solemn circle and watch as if studying the strange beast. Again and again he would rush upon them, only to find that he was fighting the wind. Mad as a hornet, he would single out a cub and follow him headlong through brush and brake till some subtle warning thrilled through his madness, telling him to heed his flank; then as he whirled he would find the savage old mother close at his heels, her white fangs bared and a dangerous flash in her eyes as she saw the hamstring so near, so easy to reach. One spring and a snap, and the ramping, masterful stag would have been helpless as a rabbit, his tendons cut cleanly at the hock; another snap and he must come down, spite of his great power, and be food for the growing cubs that sat on their tails watching him, unterrified now by his fierce challenge. But Megaleep's time had not yet come; besides, he was too tough. So the wolves studied him awhile, amused perhaps at the rough play; then, as if at a silent command, they vanished like shadows into the nearest cover, leaving the big stag in his rage to think himself master of all the world.

Sometimes as the old he-wolf ranged alone, a silent, powerful, noble-looking brute, he would meet the caribou, and there would be a fascinating bit of animal play. He rarely turned aside, knowing his own power, and the cows and fawns after one look would bound aside and rack away at a marvelous pace over the barrens. In a moment or two, finding that they were not molested, they would turn and

watch the wolf curiously till he disappeared, trying perhaps to puzzle it out why the ferocious enemy of the deep snows and the bitter cold should now be harmless as the passing birds.

Again a young bull with his keen, polished spike-horns, more active and dangerous but less confident than the over-antlered stags, would stand in the old wolf's path, disputing with lowered front the right of way. Here the right of way meant a good deal, for in many places on the high plains the scrub spruces grow so thickly that a man can easily walk over the tops of them on his snow-shoes, and the only possible passage in summer-time is by means of the numerous paths worn through the scrub by the passing of animals for untold ages. So one or the other of the two splendid brutes that now approached each other in the narrow way must turn aside or be beaten down underfoot.

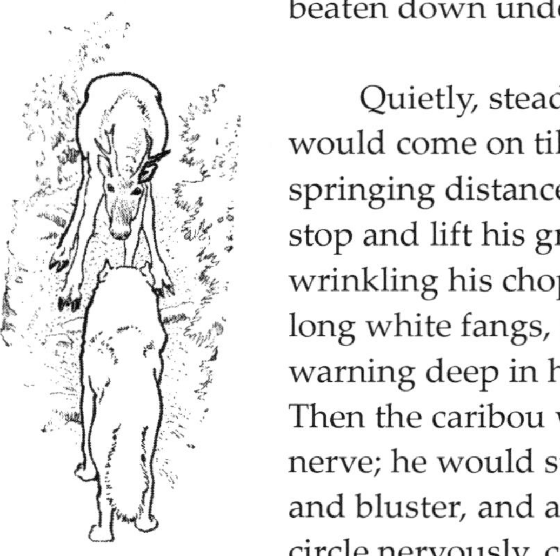

Quietly, steadily, the old wolf would come on till almost within springing distance, when he would stop and lift his great head, wrinkling his chops to show the long white fangs, and rumbling a warning deep in his massive chest. Then the caribou would lose his nerve; he would stamp and fidget and bluster, and at last begin to circle nervously, crashing his way into the scrub as if for a chance to take his enemy in the flank. Whereupon the old wolf would trot quietly along the path, paying no more heed to the interruption; while the young bull would stand wondering, his body hidden in the scrub and his head thrust into the narrow path to look after his strange adversary.

Another time, as the old wolf ranged along the edges of the barrens where the caribou herds were gathering, he would hear the challenge of a huge stag and the warning crack of twigs and the thunder of hoofs as the brute charged. Still the wolf trotted quietly along, watching from the corners of his eyes till the stag was upon him, when he sprang lightly aside and let the rush go harmlessly by. Sitting on his tail he would watch the caribou closely—and who could tell what was passing behind those cunning eyes that glowed steadily like coals, unruffled as yet by the passing winds, but ready at a rough breath to break out in flames of fire? Again and again the stag would charge, growing more furious at every failure; and every time the wolf leaped aside he left a terrible gash in his enemy's neck or side, punishing him cruelly for his bullying attack, yet strangely refusing to kill, as he might have done, or to close on the hamstring with one swift snap that would have put the big brute out of the fight forever. At last, knowing perhaps from past experience the uselessness of punishing or of disputing with this madman that felt no wounds in his rage, the wolf would lope away to cover, followed by a victorious bugle-cry that rang over the wide barren and echoed back from the mountain side. Then the wolf would circle back stealthily and put his nose down into the stag's hoof-marks for a long, deep sniff, and go quietly on his way again. A wolf's nose never forgets. When he finds that trail wandering with a score of others over the snow, in the bitter days to come when the pack are starving, Wayeeses will know whom he is following.

Besides the caribou there were other things to rouse the cubs' curiosity and give them something pleasant to do besides eating and sleeping. When the hunter's moon rose full and clear over the woods, filling all animals with strange unrest, the pack would circle the great harbor, trotting silently along, nose to tail in single file, keeping on the high ridge of mountains and looking like a distant train of husky dogs against the moonlight. When over the fishing village they would sit down, each one on the loftiest rock he could find, raise their muzzles to the stars, and join in the long howl, *Ooooooo-wow-ow-ow!* a terrible, wailing cry that seemed to drive every dog within hearing stark crazy. Out of the village lanes far below they rushed headlong, and sitting on the beach in a wide circle, heads all in and tails out, they raised their noses to the distant, wolf-topped pinnacles and joined in the wailing answer. Then the wolves would sit very still, listening with cocked ears to the cry of

their captive kinsmen, till the dismal howling died away into silence, when they would start the clamor into life again by giving the wolf's challenge.

Why they did it, what they felt there in the strange unreality of the moonlight, and what hushed their profound enmity, none can tell. Ordinarily the wolf hates both fox and dog, and kills them whenever they cross his path; but to-night the foxes were yapping an answer all around them, and sometimes a few adventurous dogs would scale the mountains silently to sit on the rocks and join in the wild wolf chorus, and not a wolf stirred to molest them. All were more or less lunatic, and knew not what they were doing.

For hours the uncanny comedy would drag itself on into the tense midnight silence, the wailing cry growing more demented and heartrending as the spell of ancient days fell again upon the degenerate huskies. Up on the lonely mountain tops the moon looked down, still and cold, and saw upon every pinnacle

a dog or a wolf, each with his head turned up at the sky, howling his heart out. Down in the hamlet, scattered for miles along Deep Arm and the harbor shore, sleepers stirred uneasily at the clamor, the women clutching their babies close, the men cursing the crazy brutes and vowing all sorts of vengeance on the morrow. Then the wolves would slip away like shadows into the vast upland barrens, and the dogs, restless as witches with some unknown excitement, would run back to whine and scratch at the doors of their masters' cabins.

Soon the big snowflakes were whirling in the air, busily weaving a soft white winding-sheet for the autumn which was passing away. And truly it had been a good time for the wolf cubs, as for most wild animals; and they had grown large and strong with their fat feeding, and wise with their many experiences. The ducks and geese vanished, driving southward ahead of the fierce autumn gales, and only the late broods of hardy eiders were left for a little season. Herring and caplin had long since drifted away into unknown depths, where the tides flowed endlessly over them and brought never a one ashore. Hares and ptarmigans turned white to hide on the snow, so that wolf and fox would pass close by without seeing them. Wood-mice pushed their winding tunnels and made their vaulted play rooms deep under the drifts, where none might molest nor make them afraid; and all game grew wary and wild, learning from experience, as it always does, that only the keen can survive the fall hunting. So the long winter, with its snow and ice and its bitter cold and its grim threat of famine, settled heavily over Harbor Weal and the Long Range where Wayeeses must find his living.

The White Wolf's Hunting

THREATENING as the northern winter was, with its stern order to the birds to depart, and to the beasts to put on their thick furs, and to the little folk of the snow to hide themselves in white coats, and to all living things to watch well the ways that they took, it could bring no terror to Wayeeses and her powerful young cubs. The gladness of life was upon them, with none of its pains or anxieties or fears, as we know them; and they rolled and tumbled about in the first deep snow with the abandon of young foxes, filled with wonder at the strange blanket that covered the rough places of earth so softly and made their light footsteps more noiseless than before. For to be noiseless and inconspicuous, and so in harmony with his surroundings, is the first desire of every creature of the vast solitudes.

Meeting the wolves now, as they roamed wild and free over the great range, one would hardly have recognized the little brown creatures that he saw playing about the den where the trail began. The cubs were already noble-looking brutes, larger than the largest husky dog; and the parents were taller, with longer legs and more massive heads and powerful jaws, than any great timber-wolf. A tremendous vitality thrilled in them from nose to paw tips. Their great bodies, as they lay quiet in the snow with heads raised and hind legs bent under them, were like powerful engines, tranquil under enormous pressure; and when they rose the movement was like the quick snap of a steel spring. Indeed, half the ordinary movements of Wayeeses are so quick that the eye cannot follow them. One instant a wolf would be lying flat on his side, his long legs outstretched on the moss, his eyes closed in the sleepy sunshine, his body limp as a hound's after a fox chase; the next instant, like the click and blink of a camera shutter, he would be standing alert on all four feet, questioning the passing breeze or looking intently into your eyes; and you could not imagine, much less follow, the recoil of twenty big electric muscles that at some subtle warning had snapped

him automatically from one position to the other. They were all snow-white, with long thick hair and a heavy mane that added enormously to their imposing appearance; and they carried their bushy tails almost straight out as they trotted along, with a slight crook near the body,—the true wolf sign that still reappears in many collies to tell a degenerate race of a noble ancestry.

After the first deep snows the family separated, led by their growing hunger and by the difficulty of finding enough game in one cover to supply all their needs. The mother and the smallest cub remained together; the two larger cubs ranged on the other side of the mountain, beating the bush and hunting into each other's mouth, as they had been trained to do; while the big he-wolf hunted successfully by himself, as he had done for years. Scattered as they were, they still kept track of each other faithfully, and in a casual way looked after one another's needs. Wherever he was, a wolf seemed to know by instinct where his fellows were hunting many miles away. When in doubt he had only to mount the highest hill and give the rallying cry, which carried an enormous distance in the still cold air, to bring the pack swiftly and silently about him.

At times, when the cubs were hungry after a

two-days fast, they would hear, faint and far away, the food cry, *yap-yap-yooo! yap-yap-yoooooo!* quivering under the stars in the tense early-morning air, and would dart away to find game freshly killed by one of the old wolves awaiting them. Again, at nightfall, a cub's hunting cry, *ooooo, ow-ow! ooooo, ow-ow!* a deep, almost musical hoot with two short barks at the end, would come singing down from the uplands; and the wolves, leaving instantly the game they were following, would hasten up to find the two cubs herding a caribou in a cleft of the rocks,—a young caribou that had lost his mother at the hands of the hunters, and that did not know how to take care of himself. And one of the cubs would hold him there, sitting on his tail in front of the caribou to prevent his escape, while the other cub called the wolves away from their own hunting to come and join the feast.

Whether this were a conscious attempt to spare the game, or to alarm it as little as need be, it is impossible to say. Certainly the wolves know, better apparently than men, that persistent hunting destroys its own object, and that caribou especially, when much alarmed by dogs or wolves or men, will take the alarm quickly, and the scattered herds, moved by a common impulse of danger, will trail far away to other ranges. That is why the wolf, unlike the less intelligent dog, hunts always in a silent, stealthy, unobtrusive way; and why he stops hunting and goes away the instant his own hunger is satisfied or another wolf kills enough for all. And that is also the probable reason why he lets the deer alone as long as he can find any other game.

This same intelligent provision was shown in another curious way. When a wolf in his wide ranging found a good hunting-ground where small game was plentiful, he would snap up a rabbit silently in the twilight and then go far away, perhaps to join the other cubs in a gambol, or to follow them to the cliffs over a fishing village and set all the dogs to howling. By day he would lie close in some thick cover, miles away from his hunting-ground. At twilight he would steal back and hunt quietly, just long enough to get his game, and then trot away again, leaving the cover as unharried as if there were not a wolf in the whole neighborhood.

Such a good hunting-ground cannot long remain hidden from other prowlers in the wilderness; and Wayeeses, who was keeping his discovery to himself, would soon cross the trail of a certain old fox returning day after day to the same good covers. No two foxes, nor mice, nor men, nor any other two animals for that matter, ever leave the same scent, —any old hound, which will hold steadily to one fox though a dozen others cross or cover his trail, will show you that plainly in a day's hunting,—and the wolf would soon know surely that the same fox was poaching every night on his own preserves while he was away. To a casual, wandering hunter he paid no attention; but this cunning poacher must be laid by the heels, else there would not be a single rabbit left in the cover. So Wayeeses, instead of hunting himself at twilight when the rabbits are stirring, would wait till midday, when the sun is warm and foxes are sleepy, and then come back to find the poacher's trail and follow it to where Eleemos was resting for the day in a sunny opening in the scrub. There Wayeeses would steal upon him from behind and put an end to his poaching; or else, if the fox used the same nest daily, as is often the case when he is not disturbed, the wolf would circle the scrub warily to find the path by which Eleemos usually came out on his night's hunting. When he found that out Wayeeses would dart away in the long, rolling gallop that carries a wolf swiftly over the roughest country without fatigue. In an hour or two he would be back again with another wolf. Then Eleemos, dozing away in the winter sunshine, would hear an unusual racket in the scrub behind him,—some heavy animal brushing about heedlessly and sniffing loudly at a cold trail. No wolf certainly, for a wolf makes no noise. So Eleemos would get down from his warm rock and slip away, stopping to look back and listen jauntily to the clumsy brute behind him, till he ran plump into the jaws of the other wolf that was watching alert and silent beside the runway.

When the snows were deep and soft the wolves took to hunting the lynxes,—big, savage, long-clawed

fighters that swarm in the interior of Newfoundland and play havoc with the small game. For a single lynx the wolves hunted in pairs, trailing the big prowler stealthily and rushing upon him from behind with a fierce uproar to startle the wits out of his stupid head and send him off headlong, as cats go, before he knew what was after him. Away he would go in mighty jumps, sinking shoulder deep, often indeed up to his tufted ears, at every plunge. After him raced the wolves, running lightly and taking advantage of the holes he had made in the soft snow, till a swift snap in his flank brought Upweekis up with a ferocious snarl to tear in pieces his pursuers.

Then began as savage a bit of fighting as the woods ever witness, teeth against talons, wolf cunning against cat ferocity. Crouched in the snow, spitting and snarling, his teeth bared and round eyes blazing and long claws aching to close in a death grip, Upweekis waited impatient as a fury for the rush. He is an ugly fighter; but he must always get close, gripping his enemy with teeth and fore claws while the hind claws get in their deadly work, kicking downward in powerful spasmodic blows and ripping everything before them. A dog would rush in now and be torn to pieces; but not so the wolves. Dancing lightly about the big lynx they would watch their chance to leap and snap, sometimes avoiding the blow of the swift paw with its terrible claws, and sometimes catching it on their heavy manes; but always a long red mark showed on the lynx's silver fur as the wolves' teeth clicked with the voice of a steel trap and they leaped aside without serious injury. As the big cat grew blind in his fury they would seize their chance like a flash and leap together; one pair of long jaws would close hard on the spine behind the tufted ears; another pair would grip a hind leg, while the wolves sprang apart and braced to hold. Then the fight was all over; and the moose birds, in pairs, came flitting in silently to see if there were not a few unconsidered trifles of the feast for them to dispose of.

Occasionally, at nightfall, the wolves' hunting cry would ring out of the woods as one of the cubs discovered three or four of the lynxes growling horribly over some game they had pulled down together. For Upweekis too, though generally a solitary fellow, often roams with a savage band of freebooters to hunt the larger animals in the bitter winter weather. No young wolf would ever run into one of these bands alone; but when the pack rolled in upon them like a tempest the lynxes would leap squalling away in a blind rush; and the two big

"The silent, appalling death-watch began"

wolves, cutting in from the ends of the charging line, would turn a lynx kit deftly aside for the cubs to hold. Then another for themselves, and the hunt was over, —all but the feast at the end of it.

When a big and cunning lynx took to a tree at the first alarm the wolves would go aside to leeward, where Upweekis could not see them, but where their noses told them perfectly all that he was doing. Then began the long game of patience, the wolves waiting for the game to come down, and the lynx waiting for the wolves to go away. Upweekis was at a disadvantage, for he could not see when he had won; and he generally came down in an hour or two, only to find the wolves hot on his trail before he had taken a dozen jumps. Whereupon he took to another tree and the game began again.

When the night was exceeding cold—and one who has not felt it can hardly imagine the bitter, killing intensity of a northern midnight in February—the wolves, instead of going away, would wait under the tree in which the lynx had taken refuge, and the silent, appalling death-watch began. A lynx, though heavily furred, cannot long remain exposed in the intense cold without moving. Moreover he must grip the branch on which he sits more or less firmly with his claws, to keep from falling; and the tense muscles, which flex the long claws to drive them into the wood, soon grow weary and numb in the bitter frost. The wolves meanwhile trot about to keep warm; while the stupid cat sits in one spot slowly perishing, and never thinks of running up and down the tree to keep himself alive. The feet grow benumbed at last, powerless to hold on any longer, and the lynx tumbles off into the wolves' jaws; or else, knowing the danger, he leaps for the nearest wolf and dies fighting.

Spite of the killing cold, the problem of keeping warm was to the wolves always a simple one. Moving along through the winter night, always on a swift, silent trot, they picked up what game came in their way, and scarcely felt the eager cold that nipped at their ears, or the wind, keen as an icicle, that strove to penetrate the shaggy white coats that covered them. When their hunger was satisfied, or when the late day came and found them still hunting hopefully, they would push their way into the thick scrub from one of the numerous paths and lie down on a nest of leaves, which even in midwinter were dry as if no snow or rain had ever fallen. There, where no wind or gale however strong could penetrate, and with the snow filling the low branches overhead and piled over them in a soft, warm blanket three feet thick, they would push their sensitive noses into their own thick fur to keep them warm, and sleep comfortably till the early twilight came and called them out again to the hunting.

At times, when not near the scrub, they would burrow deep into a great drift of snow and sleep in the warmest kind of a nest,—a trick that the husky dogs, which are

but wolves of yesterday, still remember. Like all wild animals, they felt the coming of a storm long before the first white flakes began to whirl in the air; and when a great storm threatened they would lie down to sleep in a cave, or a cranny of the rocks, and let the drifts pile soft and warm over them. However long the storm, they never stirred abroad; partly for their own comfort, partly because all game lies hid at such times and it is practically impossible, even for a wolf, to find it. When a wolf has fed full he can go a week without eating and suffer no great discomfort. So Wayeeses would lie close and warm while the snow piled deep around him and the gale raged over the sea and mountains, but passed unfelt and unheeded over his head. Then, when the storm was over, he pawed his way up through the drift and came out in a new, bright world, where the game, with appetites sharpened by the long fast, was already stirring briskly in every covert.

When March came, the bitterest month of all for the Wood Folk, even Wayeeses was often hard pressed to find a living. Small game grew scarce and very wild; the caribou had wandered far away to other ranges; and the cubs would dig for hours after a mouse, or stalk a snowbird, or wait with endless patience for a red squirrel to stop his chatter and come down to search under the snow for a fir cone that he had hidden there in the good autumn days. And once, when the hunger within was more nipping than the eager cold without, one of the cubs found a bear sleeping in his winter den among the rocks. With a sharp hunting cry, that sang like a bullet over the frozen wastes, he called the whole pack about him. While the rest lay in hiding the old he-wolf approached warily and scratched Mooween out of his den, and then ran away to entice the big brute into the open ground, where the pack rolled in upon him and killed him in a terrible fight before he had fairly shaken the sleep out of his eyes.

Old Tomah, the trapper, was abroad now, taking advantage of the spring hunger. The wolves often crossed his snow-shoe trail, or followed it swiftly to see whither it led. For a wolf, like a farm dog, is never satisfied till he knows the ways of every living thing that crosses his range. Following the broad trail Wayeeses would find here a trapped animal, struggling desperately with the clog and the cruel gripping teeth, there the flayed carcass of a lynx or an otter, and yonder the leg of a dog or a piece of caribou meat hung by a cord over a runway, with the snow disturbed beneath it where the deadly trap was hidden. One glance, or a sniff at a distance, was enough for the wolf. Lynxes do not go about the range without their skins, and meat does not naturally hang on trees; so Wayeeses, knowing all the ways of the woods, would ignore these baits absolutely. Nevertheless he followed the snow-shoe trails until he knew where every unnatural thing lay hidden; and no matter how hungry he was, or how cunningly the old Indian hid his devices, or however deep the new snow covered all traces of man's work, Wayeeses passed by on the other side and kept his dainty feet out of every snare and pitfall.

Once, when the two cubs that hunted together were hard pinched with hunger, they found Old Tomah in the twilight and followed him stealthily. The old Indian was swinging along, silent as a shadow of the woods, his gun on his shoulder and some skins on his back, heading swiftly for the little hut under the cliff, where he burrowed for the night as snug as a bear in his den. An old wolf would have known instantly the danger, for man alone bites at a distance; but the lop-eared cub, which was larger than his brother and therefore the leader, raised his head for the hunting cry. The first yap had hardly left his throat when the thunder roared, and something seared the wolf's side like a hot iron. The cubs vanished like the smoke from the old gun. Then the Indian came swiftly back on the trail, peering about with hawk eyes to see the effect of his shot.

"By cosh! miss um dat time. Mus' be powder no good." Then, as he read the plain record in the snow, "One,—by cosh! two hwulf, lil fool hwulf, follow my footin'. Mus' be more, come soon pretty quick now; else he don' howl dat way. Guess mebbe ol' Injun better stay in house nights." And he trailed warily back to hide himself behind a rock and watch till dark in front of his little *commoosie*.

Old Tomah's sleep was sound as usual that night; so he could not see the five shadows that stole out of the woods, nor hear the light footfalls that circled his camp, nor feel the breath, soft as an eddy of wind in a spruce top, that whiffed at the crack under his door and drifted away again. Next morning he saw the tracks and understood them; and as he trailed away through the still woods he was wondering, in his silent Indian way, why an old wolf should always bring Malsunsis, the cub, for a good look and a sniff at anything that he is to avoid ever after.

When all else fails follow the caribou, —that is the law which governs the wolf in the hungry days; but before they crossed the mountains and followed the long valleys to the far southern ranges the wolves went back to the hills, where the trail began, for a more exciting and dangerous kind of hunting. The pack had held closer together of late; for the old wolves must often share even a scant fox or rabbit with the hungry and inexperienced youngsters. Now, when famine drove them to the very doors of the one enemy to be feared, only the wisest and wariest old wolf was fit to lead the foray.

The little fishing village was buried under drifts and almost deserted. A few men lingered to watch the boats and houses; but the families had all gone inland to the winter tilts for wood and shelter. By night the wolves would come stealthily to prowl among the deserted lanes; and the fishermen, asleep in their clothes under caribou skins, or sitting close by the stove behind barred doors, would know nothing of the huge, gaunt forms that flitted noiselessly past the frosted windows. If a pig were left in his pen a sudden terrible squealing would break out on the still night; and when the fisherman rushed out the pen would be empty, with nothing whatever to account for piggie's disappearance. For to their untrained eyes even the tracks of the wolves were covered up by those of the numerous big huskies. If a cat prowled abroad, or an uneasy dog scratched to be let out, there would be a squall, a yelp,—and the cat would not come back, and the dog would never scratch at the door to be let in again.

Only when nothing stirred in the village, when the dogs and cats had been spirited away, and when not even a rat stole from under the houses to gnaw at a fishbone, would the fishermen know of their big silent visitors. Then the wolves would gather on a snow-drift just outside the village and raise a howl, a frightful wail of famine and disappointment, that made the air shudder. From within the houses the dogs answered with mad clamor. A door would open to show first a long seal gun, then a fisherman, then a fool dog that darted between the fisherman's legs and capered away, ki-yi-ing a challenge to the universe. A silence, tense as a bowstring; a sudden yelp—*Hui-hui*, as the fisherman whistled to the dog that was being whisked away over the snow with a grip on his throat that prevented any answer; then the fisherman would wait and call in vain, and shiver, and go back to the fire again.

Almost every pleasant day a train of dogs would leave the village and go far back on the hills to haul fire-wood, or poles for the new fish-flakes. The wolves, watching from their old den, would follow at a distance to pick up a careless dog that ventured away from the fire to hunt rabbits when his harness was taken off. Occasionally a solitary wood-chopper would start with sudden alarm as a big white form glided into sight, and the alarm would be followed by genuine terror as he found himself surrounded by five huge wolves that sat on their tails watching him curiously. Gripping his ax he would hurry back to call his companions and harness the dogs and hurry back to the village before the early darkness should fall upon them. As the komatik went careering over the snow, the dogs yelping and straining at the harness, the men running alongside shouting *Hi-hi* and cracking their whips, they could still see, over their shoulders, the wolves following lightly close behind; but when they rushed breathless into their houses, and grabbed their guns, and ran back on the trail, there was nothing to be seen. For the wolves, quick as light to feel the presence of danger, were already far away, trotting swiftly up the frozen arm of the harbor, following another sledge trail which came down that morning from the wilderness.

That same night the wolves appeared silently in the little lodge, far up the Southeast Brook, where in a sheltered hollow of the hills the fishermen's families were sleeping away the bitter winter. Here for one long night they watched and waited in vain; for every living thing was safe in the tilts behind barred doors. In the morning little Noel's eyes kindled as he saw the wolves' tracks; and when they came back again the tilts were watching. As the lop-eared cub darted after a cat that shot like a ray of moonlight under a cabin, a window opened noiselessly, and *zing!* a bowstring twanged its sharp warning in the tense silence. With a yelp the wolf tore the arrow from his shoulder. The warm blood followed the barb, and he lapped it eagerly in his hunger. Then, as the danger swept over him, he gave the trail cry and darted away. Doors

banged open here and there; dogs barked to crack their throats; seal guns roared out and sent their heavy echoes crashing like thunder among the hills. Silence fell again over the lodge; and there were left only a few frightened dogs whose noses had already told them everything, a few fishermen who watched and listened, and one Indian boy with a long bow in his hand and an arrow ready on the string, who trailed away with a little girl at his side trying to puzzle out the track of one wolf that left a drop of blood here and there on the snow in the scant moonlight.

Far up on the hillside in a little opening of the woods the scattered pack came together again. At the first uproar, so unbearable to a silence-loving animal, they had vanished in five different directions; yet so subtle, so perfect is the instinct which holds a wolf family together that the old mother had scarcely entered the glade alone and sat down to wait and listen when the other wolves joined her silently. Malsunsis, the big cub, scarcely felt his wound at first, for the arrow had but glanced through the thick skin and flesh, and he had torn it out without difficulty; but the old he-wolf limped painfully and held up one fore leg, pierced by a seal shot, as he loped away over the snow.

It was their first rough experience with men, and probably the one feeling in every shaggy head was of puzzled wonder as to how and why it had all happened. Hitherto they had avoided men with a certain awe, or watched them curiously at a distance, trying to understand their superior ways; and never a hostile feeling for the masters of the woods had found place in a wolf's breast. Now man had spoken at last; his voice was a brutal command to be gone, and curiously enough these powerful big brutes, any one of which could have pulled down a man more easily than a caribou, never thought of questioning the order.

It was certainly time to follow the caribou—that was probably the one definite purpose that came upon the wolves, sitting in a silent, questioning circle in the moonlight, with only the deep snows and the empty woods around them. For a week they had not touched food; for thrice that time they had not fed full, and a few days more would leave them unable to cope with the big caribou, which are always full fed and strong, thanks to nature's abundance of deer moss on the barrens. So they started as by a single impulse, and the mother wolf led them swiftly southward, hour after hour at a tireless pace, till the great he-wolf weakened and turned aside to nurse his wounded fore leg. The lop-eared cub drew out of the race at the same time. His own wound now required the soft massage of his tongue to allay the fever; and besides, the fear that was born in him, one night long ago, and that had slept ever since, was now awake again, and for the first time he was afraid to face the famine and the wilderness alone. So the pack swept on, as if their feet would never tire, and the two wounded wolves crept into the scrub and lay down together.

A strange, terrible feeling stole swiftly over the covert, which had always hitherto been a place of rest and quiet content. The cub was licking his wound softly when he looked up in sudden alarm, and there was the great he-wolf looking at him hungrily, with a frightful flare in his green eyes. The cub moved away startled and tried to soothe his wound again; but the uncanny feeling was strong upon him still, and when he turned his head there was the big wolf, which had crept forward till he could see the cub behind a twisted spruce root, watching him steadily with the same horrible stare in his unblinking eyes. The hackles rose up on the cub's neck and a growl rumbled in his deep chest, for he knew now what it all meant. The smell of blood was in the air, and the old he-wolf, that had so often shared his kill to save the cubs, was now going crazy in his awful hunger. Another moment and there would have been a terrible duel in the scrub; but as the wolves sprang to their feet and faced each other some deep, unknown feeling stirred within them and they turned aside. The old wolf threw himself down heavily, facing away from the temptation, and the cub slipped aside to find another den, out of sight and smell of the huge leader, lest the scent of blood should overcome them again and cause them to fly at each other's throats in uncontrollable fury.

Next morning a queer thing happened, but not uncommon under the circumstances among wolves and huskies. The cub was lying motionless, his head on his paws, his eyes wide open, when something stirred near him. A red squirrel came scampering through the scrub branches just under the thick coating of snow that filled all their tops. Slowly, carefully the young wolf gathered his feet under him, tense as a bowstring. As the squirrel whisked overhead the wolf leaped like a flash, caught him, and crushed him with a single grip. Then with the squirrel in his mouth he made his way back to where the big leader was lying, his head on his paws, his eyes turned aside. Slowly, warily the cub approached, with a friendly twist of his ears and head, till he laid the squirrel at the big wolf's very nose, then drew back a step and lay with paws extended and tail thumping the leaves, watching till the tidbit was seized ravenously and crushed and bolted in a single mouthful. Next instant both wolves sprang to their feet and made their way out of the scrub together.

They took up the trail of the pack where they had left it, and followed it ten hours, the cub at a swift trot, the old wolf loping along on three legs. Then a rest, and forward again, slower and slower, night after day in ever-failing strength, till on the edge of a great barren they stopped as if struck, trembling all over as the reek of game poured into their starving nostrils.

Too weak now to kill or to follow the fleet caribou, they lay down in the snow waiting, their ears cocked, their noses questioning every breeze for its good news. Left to themselves the trail must end here, for they could go no farther; but somewhere ahead in the vast silent barren the cubs were trailing, and somewhere beyond them the old mother wolf was laying her ambush.—Hark! from a spur of the valley, far below on their left, rang out the food cry, singing its way in the frosty air over woods and plains, and hurrying back over the trail to tell those who had fallen by the way that they were not forgotten. And when they leaped up, as at an electric shock, and raced for the cry, there were the cubs and the mother wolf, their hunger already satisfied, and there in the snow a young bull caribou to save them.

So the long, hard winter passed away, and

The White Wolf's Hunting

spring came again with its abundance. Grouse drummed a welcome in the woods; the *honk* of wild geese filled the air with a joyous clangor, and in every open pool the ducks were quacking. No need now to cling like shadows to the herds of caribou, and no further need for the pack to hold together. The ties that held them melted like snows in the sunny hollows. First the old wolves, then the cubs, one by one drifted away whither the game or their new mates were calling them. When the summer came there was another den on the high hill overlooking the harbor, where the little brown cubs could look down with wonder at the shining sea and the slow fishing-boats and the children playing on the shore; but the wolves whose trail began there were far away over the mountains, following their own ways, waiting for the crisp hunting cry that should bring them again together.

TRAILS THAT CROSS
IN THE SNOW

Trails that Cross in the Snow

"ARE we lost, little brother?" said Mooka, shivering.

No need of the question, startling and terrible as it was from the lips of a child astray in the vast solitudes; for a great gale had swooped down from the Arctic, blotting out in clouds of whirling snow the world of plain and mountain and forest that, a moment before, had stretched wide and still before the little hunters' eyes.

For an hour or more, running like startled deer, they had tried to follow their own snow-shoe trail back over the wide barrens into the friendly woods; but already the snow had filled it brim full, and whatever faint trace was left of the long raquettes was caught up by the gale and whirled away with a howl of exultation. Before them as they ran every trail of wolf and caribou and snow-shoe, and every distant landmark, had vanished; the world was but a chaos of mad rolling snow clouds; and behind them—Their stout little hearts trembled as they saw not a vestige of the trail they had just made. With the great world itself, their own little tracks, as fast as they made them, were swept and blotted out of existence. Like two sparrows that had dropped blinded and bewildered on the vast plain out of the snow cloud, they huddled together without one friendly sign to tell them whence they had come or whither they were going. Worst of all, the instinct of direction, which often guides an Indian through the still fog or the darkest night, seemed benumbed by the cold and the tumult; and not even Old Tomah himself could have told north or south in the blinding storm.

Still they ran on bravely, bending to the fierce blasts, heading the wind as best they could, till Mooka, tripping a second time in a little hollow where a brook ran deep under the snow, and knowing now that they were but wandering in an endless circle, seized Noel's arm and repeated her question:

"Are we lost, little brother?"

And Noel, lost and bewildered, but gripping his bow in his fur mitten and peering here and there, like an old hunter, through the whirling flakes and rolling gusts to catch some landmark, some lofty crag or low tree-line that held steady in the mad dance of the world, still made confident Indian answer:

"Noel not lost; Noel right here. Camp lost, little sister."

"Can we find um, little brother?"

"Oh, yes, we find um. Find um bimeby, pretty soon quick now, after storm."

"But storm last all night, and it's soon dark. Can we rest and not freeze? Mooka tired and—and frightened, little brother."

"Sartin we rest; build um *commoosie* and sleep jus' like bear in his den. Oh, yes, sartin we rest good," said Noel cheerfully.

"And the wolves, little brother?" whispered Mooka, looking back timidly into the wild waste out of which they had come.

"Never mind hwolves; nothing hunts in storm, little sister. Come on, we must find um woods now." For one brief moment the little hunter stood with upturned face, while Mooka bowed her head silently, and the great storm rolled unheeded over them. Still holding his long bow he stretched both hands to the sky in the mute appeal that *Keesuolukh*, the Great Mystery whom we call God, would understand better than all words. Then turning their backs to the gale they drifted swiftly away before it, like two wind-blown leaves, running to keep from freezing, and holding each other's hands tight lest they separate and be lost by the way.

The second winter had come, sealing up the gloomy land till it rang like iron at the touch, then covering it deep with snow and polishing its mute white face with hoar-frost and hail driven onward by the fierce Arctic gales. An appalling silence rested on plains and mountains. Not a chirp, not a rustle broke the intense, unnatural stillness. One might travel all day long without a sight or sound of life; and when the early twilight came and life stirred shyly from its coverts and snow caves, the Wood Folk stole out into the bare white world on noiseless, hesitating feet, as if in presence of the dead.

When the Moon of Famine came, the silence was rudely broken. Before daylight one morning, when the air was so tense and still that a whisper set it tinkling like silver bells, the rallying cry of the wolves rolled down from a mountain top; and the three cubs, that had waited long for the signal, left their separate trails far away and hurried to join the old leader.

When the sun rose that morning one who stood on the high ridge of the Top Gallants, far to the eastward of Harbor Weal, would have seen seven trails winding down among the rocks and thickets. It needed only a glance to show that the seven trails, each one as clear-cut and delicate as that of a prowling fox, were the records of wolves' cautious feet; and that they were no longer beating the thickets for grouse and rabbits, but moving swiftly all together for the edges of the vast barrens where the caribou herds were feeding. Another glance —but here we must have the cunning eyes of Old Tomah the hunter—would have told that two of the trails were those of enormous wolves which led the pack; two others were plainly cubs that had not yet lost the cub trick of frolicking in the soft snow; while three others were just wolves, big and powerful brutes that moved as if on steel springs, and that still held to the old pack because the

time had not yet come for them to scatter finally to their separate ways and head new packs of their own in the great solitudes.

Out from the woods on the other side of the barren came two snow-shoe trails, which advanced with short steps and rested lightly on the snow, as if the makers of the trails were little people whose weight on the snow-shoes made hardly more impression than the broad pads of Moktaques the rabbit. They followed stealthily the winding records of a score of caribou that had wandered like an eddying wind all over the barren, stopping here and there to paw great holes in the snow for the caribou moss that covered all the earth beneath. Out at the end of the trail two Indian children, a girl and a boy, stole along with noiseless steps, scanning the wide wastes for a cloud of mist—the frozen breath that hovers over a herd of caribou—or peering keenly into the edges of the woods for vague white shapes moving like shadows among the trees. So they moved on swiftly, silently, till the boy stopped with a startled exclamation, whipped out a long arrow with a barbed steel point, and laid it ready across his bow. For at his feet was another light trail, the trail of a wolf pack, that crossed his own, moving straight and swift across the barren toward the unseen caribou.

Just in front, as the boy stopped, a slight motion broke the even white surface that stretched away silent and lifeless on every side,—a motion so faint and natural that Noel's keen eyes, sweeping the plain and the edges of the distant woods, never noticed it. A vagrant wind, which had been wandering and moaning all morning as if lost, seemed to stir the snow and settle to rest again. But now, where the plain seemed most empty and lifeless, seven great white wolves crouched down in the snow in a little hollow, their paws extended, their hind legs bent like powerful springs beneath them, their heads raised cautiously so that only their ears and eyes showed above the rim of the little hollow where they hid. So they lay, tense, alert, ready, watching with eager, inquisitive eyes the two children drawing steadily nearer, the only sign of life in the whole wide, desolate landscape.

Follow the back trail of the snow-shoes now, while the wolves are waiting, and it leads you over the great barren into the gloomy spruce woods; beyond that it crosses two more barrens and stretches of intervening forest; then up a great hill and down into a valley, where the lodge lay hidden, buried deep under Newfoundland snows.

Here the fishermen lived, sleeping away the bitter winter. In the late autumn they had left the fishing village at Harbor

Weal, driven out like the wild ducks by the fierce gales that raged over the whole coast. With their abundant families and scant provisions they had followed the trail up the Southwest Brook till it doubled around the mountain and led into a great silent wood, sheltered on every side by the encircling hills. Here the tilts were built with double walls, filled in between with leaves and moss, to help the little stoves that struggled bravely with the terrible cold; and the roofs were covered over with poles and bark, or with the brown sails that had once driven the fishing-boats out and in on the wings of the gale. The high mountains on the west stood between them and the icy winds that swept down over the sea from the Labrador and the Arctic wastes; wood in abundance was at their doors, and the trout-stream that sang all day long under its bridges of snow and ice was always ready to brim their kettles out of its abundance.

So the new life began pleasantly enough; but as the winter wore away and provisions grew scarce and game vanished from the coverts, they all felt the fearful pinch of famine. Every morning now a confused circle of tracks in the snow showed where the wild prowlers of the woods had come and sniffed at the very doors of the tilts in their ravening hunger.

Noel's father and Old Tomah were far away, trapping, in the interior; and to Noel with his snares and his bow and arrows fell the pleasant task of supplying the family's need when the stock of dried fish melted away. On this March morning he had started with Mooka at daylight to cross the mountains to some great barrens where he had found tracks and knew that a few herds of caribou were still feeding. The sun was dimmed as it rose, and the sun-dogs gave mute warning of the coming storm; but the cupboard was empty at home, and even a little hunter thinks first of the game he is following and lets the storm take care of itself. So they hurried on unheeding,—Noel with his bow and arrows, Mooka with a little bag containing a loaf and a few dried caplin,—peering under every brush pile for the shining eyes of a rabbit, and picking up one big grouse and a few ptarmigan among the bowlders of a great bare hillside. On the edges of the great barren under the Top Gallants they found the fresh tracks of feeding caribou, and were following eagerly when they ran plump into the wolf trail.

Now by every law of the chase the game belonged to these earlier hunters; and by every power in their gaunt, famished bodies the wolves meant to have it. So said the trail. Every stealthy advance in single file across, the open, every swift rush over the hollows that might hide them from eyes watching back from the distant woods, showed the wolves' purpose clear as daylight; and had Noel been wiser he would have read a warning from the snow and turned aside. But he only drew his longest, keenest arrow and pressed on more eagerly than before.

The two trails had crossed each other at last. Beginning near together, one on the mountains, the other by the sea, they had followed their separate devious ways, now far apart in the glad bright summer, now drawing together in the moonlight of the winter's night. At times the makers of the trails had watched each other in secret, shyly, inquisitively, at a distance; but always fear or cunning had kept them apart, the boy with his keen hunter's interest baffled and whetted by the brutes' wariness, and the wolves drawn to the superior being by that subtle instinct that once made glad hunting-dogs and collies of the wild rangers of the plains, and that still leads a wolf to follow and watch the doings of men with intense curiosity. Now the trails had met fairly in the snow, and a few steps more would bring the boy and the wolf face to face.

Noel was stealing along warily, his arrow ready on the string. Mooka beside him was watching a faint cloud of mist, the breath of caribou, that blurred at times the dark tree-line in the distance, when one of those mysterious warnings that befall the hunter in the far North rested upon them suddenly like a heavy hand.

I know not what it is,—what lesser pressure of air, to which we respond like a barometer; or what unknown chords there are within us that sleep for years in the midst of society and that waken and answer, like an animal's, to the subtle influence of nature,—but one can never be watched by an unseen wild animal without feeling it vaguely; and one can never be so keen on the trail that the storm, before it breaks, will not whisper a warning to turn back to shelter before it is too late. To Noel and Mooka, alone on the barrens, the sun was no dimmer than before; the heavy gray bank of clouds still held sullenly to its place on the horizon; and no eyes, however keen, would have noticed the tiny dark spots that centered and glowed upon them over the rim of the little hollow where the wolves were watching. Nevertheless, a sudden chill fell upon them both. They stopped abruptly, shivering a bit, drawing closer together and scanning the waste keenly to know what it all meant.

"*Mitcheegeesookh,* the storm!" said Noel sharply; and without another word they turned and hurried back on their own trail. In a short half hour the world would be swallowed up in chaos. To be caught out on the barrens meant to be lost; and to be lost here without fire and shelter meant death, swift and sure. So they ran on, hoping to strike the woods before the blizzard burst upon them.

They were scarcely half-way to shelter when the white flakes began to whirl around them. With startling, terrible swiftness the familiar world vanished; the guiding trail was blotted out, and nothing but a wolf's instinct could have held a straight course in the blinding fury of the storm. Still they held on bravely, trying in vain to keep their direction by the eddying winds, till Mooka stumbled twice at the same hollow over a hidden brook, and they knew they were running blindly in a circle of death. Frightened at the discovery they turned, as the caribou do, keeping their backs steadily to the winds, and drifted slowly away down the long barren.

Hour after hour they struggled on, hand in hand, without a thought of where they were going. Twice Mooka fell and lay still, but was dragged to her feet and hurried onward again. The little hunter's own strength was almost gone, when a low moan rose steadily above the howl and hiss of the gale. It was the spruce woods, bending their tops to the blast and groaning at the strain. With a wild whoop Noel plunged forward, and the next instant they were safe within the woods. All around them the flakes sifted steadily, silently down into the thick covert, while the storm passed with a great roar over their heads.

In the lee of a low-branched spruce they stopped again, as though by a common impulse, while Noel lifted his hands. "Thanks, thanks, *Keesuolukh*; we can take care of ourselves now," the brave little heart was singing under the upstretched arms. Then they tumbled into the snow and lay for a moment utterly relaxed, like two tired animals, in that brief, delicious rest which follows a terrible struggle with the storm and cold.

First they ate a little of their bread and fish to keep up their spirits; then—for the storm that was upon them might last for days—they set about preparing a shelter. With a little search, whooping to each other lest they stray away, they found a big dry stub that some gale had snapped off a few feet above the snow. While Mooka scurried about, collecting birch bark and armfuls of dry branches, Noel took off his snow-shoes and began with one of them to shovel away the snow in a semicircle around the base of the stub. In a short half-hour he had a deep hole there, with the snow banked up around it to the height of his head. Next with his knife he cut a lot of light poles and scrub spruces and, sticking the butts in his snowbank, laid the tops, like the sticks of a wigwam, firmly against the big stub. A few armfuls of spruce boughs shingled over this roof, and a few minutes' work shoveling snow thickly upon them to hold them in place and to make a warm covering; then a doorway, or rather a narrow tunnel, just beyond the stub on the straight side of the semicircle, and their *commoosie* was all ready. Let the storm roar and the snow sift down! The thicker it fell the warmer would be their shelter. They laughed and shouted now as they scurried out and in, bringing boughs for a bed and the fire-wood which Mooka had gathered.

Against the base of the dry stub they built their fire,—a wee, sociable little fire such as an Indian always builds, which is far better than a big one, for it draws you near and welcomes you cheerily, instead of driving you away by its smoke and great heat. Soon the big stub itself began to burn, glowing steadily with a heat that filled the snug little *commoosie*, while the smoke found its way out of the hole in the roof which Noel had left for that purpose. Later the stub burned through to its hollow center, and then they had a famous chimney, which soon grew hot and glowing inside, and added its mite to the children's comfort.

Noel and Mooka were drowsy now; but before the long night closed in upon them they had gathered more wood, and laid aside some wisps of birch bark to use when they should wake, cold and shivering, and find their little fire gone out and the big stub losing its cheery glow. Then they lay down to rest, and the night and the storm rolled on unheeded.

Towards morning they fell into a heavy sleep; for the big stub began to burn more freely as the wind changed, and they need not stir every half hour to feed their little fire and keep from freezing. It was broad daylight, the storm had ceased, and a woodpecker was hammering loudly on a hollow shell over their heads when they started up, wondering vaguely where they were. Then while Noel broke out of the *commoosie*, which was fairly buried under the snow, to find out where he was, Mooka rebuilt the fire and plucked a ptarmigan and set it to toasting with the last of their bread over the coals.

Noel came back soon with a cheery whoop to tell the little cook that they had drifted before the storm down the whole length of the great barren, and were camped now on the opposite side, just under the highest ridge of the Top Gallants. There was not a track on the barrens, he said; not a sign of wolf or caribou, which had probably wandered deeper into the woods for shelter. So they ate their bread to the last crumb and their bird to the last bone, and, giving up all thought of hunting, started up the big barren, heading for the distant Lodge, where they had long since been given up for lost.

They had crossed the barren and a mile of thick woods beyond when they ran into the fresh trail of a dozen caribou. Following it swiftly they came to the edge of a much smaller barren that they had crossed yesterday, and saw at a glance that the trail stretched straight across it. Not a caribou was in sight; but they might nevertheless be feeding, or resting in the woods just beyond; and for the little hunters to show

themselves now in the open would mean that they would become instantly the target for every keen eye that was watching the back trail. So they started warily to circle the barren, keeping just within the fringe of woods out of sight.

They had gone scarcely a hundred steps when Noel whipped out a long arrow and pointed silently across the open. From the woods on the other side the caribou had broken out of a dozen tunnels under the spruces, and came trotting back in their old trails, straight downwind to where the little hunters were hiding.

The deer were acting queerly,—now plunging away with the high, awkward jumps that caribou use when startled; now swinging off on their swift, tireless rack, and before they had settled to their stride halting suddenly to look back and wag their ears at the trail. For Megaleep is full of curiosity as a wild turkey, and always stops to get a little entertainment out of every new thing that does not threaten him with instant death. Then out of the woods behind them trotted five white wolves, —not hunting, certainly! for whenever the caribou stopped to look the wolves sat down on their tails and yawned. One lay down and rolled over and over in the soft snow; another chased and capered after his own brush, whirling round and round like a little whirlwind, and the shrill *ki-yi* of a cub wolf playing came faintly across the barren.

It was a strange scene, yet one often witnessed on the lonely plains of the far North: the caribou halting, running away, and halting again to look back and watch the queer antics of their big enemies, which seemed now so playful and harmless; the cunning wolves playing on the game's curiosity at every turn, knowing well that if once frightened the deer would break away at a pace which would make pursuit hopeless. So they followed rather than drove the foolish deer across the barren, holding them with monkey tricks and kitten's capers, and restraining with an iron grip their own fearful hunger and the blind impulse to rush in headlong and have it all quickly over.

Kneeling behind a big spruce, Noel was trying nervously the spring and temper of his long bow, divided in desire between the caribou, which they needed sadly at home, and one of the great wolves whose death would give him a place among the mighty hunters, when Mooka clutched his arm, her eyes snapping with excitement, her finger pointing silently back on their own trail. A vague shadow glided swiftly among the trees. An enormous white wolf appeared, vanished, came near them again, and crouched down under a low spruce branch waiting.

Again the two trails had crossed in the snow. The big wolf as he appeared had thrust his nose into the snow-shoe tracks, and a sniff or two told him everything,— who had passed, and how long ago, and what they were doing, and how far ahead they were now waiting. But the caribou were coming, coaxed along marvelously by the cubs and the old mother; and the great silent wolf, that had left the pack playing with the game while he circled the barren at top speed, now turned to the business in hand with no thought nor fear of harm from the two children whom he had watched but yesterday.

Not so Noel. The fire blazed out in his eyes; the long bow swung to the wolf, bending like a steel spring, and the feathered shaft of an arrow lay close against the boy's cheek. But Mooka caught his arm—

"Look, Noel, his ear! *Malsunsis*, my little wolf cub," she breathed excitedly. And Noel, with a great wonder in his eyes, slacked his bow, while his thoughts jumped far away to the den on the mountains where the trail began, and to three little cubs playing like kittens with the grasshoppers and the cloud shadows; for the great wolf that lay so still near them, his eyes fixed in a steady glow upon the coming caribou, had one ear bent sharply forward, like a leaf that has been creased between the fingers.

"A quick snap where the heart lay"

Again Mooka broke the tense silence in a low whisper. "How many wolf trails you see yesterday, little brother?"

"Seven," said Noel, whose eyes already had the cunning of Old Tomah's to understand everything.

"Then where tother wolf? Only six here," breathed Mooka, looking timidly all around, fearing to find the steady glare of green eyes fixed upon them from the shadow of every thicket.

Noel stirred uneasily. Somewhere close at hand another huge wolf was waiting; and a wholesome fear fell upon him, with a shiver at the thought of how near he had come in his excitement to bringing the whole savage pack snarling about his ears.

A snort of alarm cut short his thinking. There at the edge of the wood, not twenty feet away, stood a caribou, pointing his ears at the children whom he had almost stumbled over as he ran, thinking only of the wolves behind. The long bow sprang back of itself; an arrow buzzed like a wasp and buried itself deep in the white chest. Like a flash a second arrow followed as the stag turned away, and with a jump or two he sank to his knees, as if to rest awhile in the snow.

But Mooka scarcely saw these things. Her eyes were fastened on the great white wolf which she had claimed for her own when he was a toddling cub. He lay still as a stone under the tip of a bending spruce branch, his eyes following every motion of a young bull caribou which three of the wolves had singled out of the herd and were now guiding surely straight to his hiding-place.

The snort and plunge of the smitten animal startled this young stag and he turned aside from his course. Like a shadow the big wolf that Mooka was watching changed his place so as to head the game, while two of the pack on the open barrens slipped around the caribou and turned him back again to the woods. At the edge of the cover the stag stopped for a last look, pointing his ears first at Noel's caribou, which now lay very still in the snow, then at the wolves, which with quick instinct had singled him out of the herd, knowing in some subtle way he was watched from beyond, and which gathered about him in a circle, sitting on their tails and yawning. Slowly, silently Mooka's wolf crept forward, pushing his great body through the snow. A terrific rush, a quick snap under the stag's chest just behind the fore legs, where the heart lay; then the big wolf leaped aside and sat down quietly again to watch.

It was soon finished. The stag plunged away, settled into his long rack, slowed down to a swaying, weakening trot. After him at a distance glided the big wolf, lapping eagerly at the crimson trail, but

holding himself with tremendous will power from rushing in headlong and driving the game, which might run for miles if too hard pressed. The stag sank to his knees; a sharp yelp rang like a pistol-shot through the still woods; then the pack rolled in like a whirlwind, and it was all over.

Creeping near on the trail the little hunters crouched under a low spruce, watching as if fascinated the wild feast of the wolves. Noel's bow was ready in his hand; but luckily the sight of these huge, powerful brutes overwhelmed him and drove all thoughts of killing out of his head. Mooka plucked him by the sleeve at last, and pointed silently homewards. It was surely time to go, for the biggest wolf had already stretched himself and was licking his paws, while the two cubs with full stomachs were rolling over and over and biting each other playfully in the snow. Silently they stole away, stopping only to tie a rag to a pointed stick, which they thrust between their own caribou's ribs to make the wolves suspicious and keep them from tearing the game and eating the tidbits while the little hunters hurried away to bring the men with their guns and dog sledges.

They had almost crossed the second barren when Mooka, looking back uneasily from the edge of the woods, saw a single big wolf emerge across the barren and follow swiftly on their trail. Startled at the sight, they turned swiftly to run; for that terrible feeling which sweeps over a hunter, when for the first time he finds himself hunted in his turn, had clutched their little hearts and crushed all their confidence. A sudden panic seized them; they rushed away for the woods, running side by side till they broke into the fringe of evergreen that surrounded the barren. There they dropped breathless under a low fir and turned to look.

"It was wrong to run, little brother," whispered Mooka.

"Why?" said Noel.

"Cause Wayeeses see it, and think we 'fraid."

"But I was 'fraid out there, little sister," confessed Noel bravely. "Here we can climb tree; good chance shoot um with my arrows."

Like two frightened rabbits they crouched under the fir, staring back with wild round eyes over the trail, fearing every instant to see the savage pack break out of the woods and come howling after them. But only the single big wolf appeared, trotting quietly along in their footsteps. Within bowshot he stopped with head raised, looking, listening intently. Then, as if he had seen them in their hiding, he turned aside, circled widely to the left, and entered the woods far below.

Again the two little hunters hurried on through the silent, snow-filled woods, a strange disquietude settling upon them as they felt they were followed by unseen feet. Soon the feeling grew too strong to resist. Noel with his bow ready, and a strange chill trickling like cold water along his spine, was hiding behind a tree watching the back trail, when a low exclamation from Mooka made him turn. There behind them, not ten steps away, a huge white wolf was sitting quietly on his tail, watching them with absorbed, silent intentness.

Fear and wonder, and swift memories of Old Tomah and the wolf that had followed him when he was lost, swept over Noel in a flood. He rose swiftly, the long bow bent, and again a deadly arrow cuddled softly against his cheek; but there were doubts and fears in his eye till Mooka caught his arm with a glad little laugh—

"My cub, little brother. See his ear, and oh, his tail! Watch um tail, little brother." For at the first move the big wolf sprang alertly to his feet, looked deep into Mooka's eyes with that intense, penetrating light which serves a wild animal to read your very thoughts, and instantly his great bushy tail was waving its friendly greeting.

It was indeed Malsunsis, the cub. Before the great storm broke he had crouched with the pack in the hollow just in front of the little hunters; and although the wolves were hungry, it was with feelings of curiosity only that they watched the children, who seemed to the powerful brutes hardly more to be feared than a couple of snowbirds hopping across the vast barren. But they were children of men—that was enough for the white-wolf packs, which for untold years had never been known to molest a man. This morning Malsunsis had again crossed their trail. He had seen them lying in wait for the caribou that his own pack were driving; had seen Noel smite the bull, and was filled with wonder; but his own business kept him still in hiding. Now, well fed and good-natured, but more curious than ever, he had followed the trail of these little folk to learn something about them.

Mooka as she watched him was brim full of an eagerness which swept away all fear. "Tomah says, wolf and Injun hunt just alike; keep ver' still; don't trouble game 'cept when he hungry," she whispered. "Says too, *Keesuolukh* made us friends 'fore white man come, spoil um everything. Das what Malsunsis say now wid hees tail and eyes; only way he can talk um, little brother. No, no,"—for Noel's bow was still strongly bent,—"you must not shoot. Malsunsis think

we friends." And trusting her own brave little heart she stepped in front of the deadly arrow and walked straight to the big wolf, which moved aside timidly and sat down again at a distance, with the friendly expression of a lost collie in eyes and ears and wagging tail tip.

Cheerfully enough Noel slacked his long bow, for the wonder of the woods was strong upon him, and the hunting-spirit, which leads one forth to frighten and kill and to break the blessed peace, had vanished in the better sense of comradeship which steals over one when he watches the Wood Folk alone and friendly in the midst of the solitudes. As they went on their way again the big wolf trotted after them, keeping close to their trail but never crossing it, and occasionally ranging up alongside, as if to keep them in the right way. Where the woods were thickest Noel, with no trail to guide him, swung uncertainly to left and right, peering through the trees for some landmark on the distant hills. Twice the big wolf trotted out to one side, returned and trotted out again in the same direction; and Noel, taking the subtle hint, as an Indian always does, bore steadily to the right till the great ridge, beyond which the Lodge was hidden, loomed over the tree-tops. And to this day he believes—and it is impossible, for I have tried, to dissuade him—that the wolf knew where they were going and tried in his own way to show them.

So they climbed the long ridge to the summit, and from the deep valley beyond the smoke of the Lodge rose up to guide them. There the wolf stopped; and though Noel whistled and Mooka called cheerily, as they would to one of their own huskies that they had learned to love, Malsunsis would go no farther. He sat there on the ridge, his tail sweeping a circle in the snow behind him, his ears cocked to the friendly call and his eyes following every step of the little hunters, till they vanished in the woods below. Then he turned to follow his own way in the wilderness.

In Quest of
Waptonk
the Wild

In Quest of Waptonk the Wild

A VAST and lonely barren, covered deep with soft-colored mosses and surrounded by gloomy spruce woods, lies basking in the early morning sunshine. The first sea-wind has just come to call it, swinging a fragrant censer over the earth and rolling up the mists that have covered it all night long. Under this fleecy, vanishing coverlet the plain seems to stir and breathe deep of the morning incense and then stretch itself drowsily, like a gray wolf just awake. Here and there little ponds or flashets of shallow water blink and quiver in the lightlike sleepy eyes, or rest in soft winding shadows like the features and wrinkles of a great weather-beaten face. Silence broods over it taking visible shape in the form of a solitary woods raven that hangs motionless high in air on sable outstretched wings. No sign of life moves on the tranquil face of the earth or water; no sound breaks the restful stillness save the cheeping of young plover hiding in the gray moss, and a low surge, like a sound in a dream, drifting in over distant woods

from where the waves break ranks on the unnamed shoals. And here—unexpectedly, as good things come at last—was the end of my long quest to find the home of Waptonk the wild goose.

Ever since childhood I had sought him. In the spring he had always called to me from the high heavens; and something in the ring of his bugle-call, something in the sight of that living arrow-head driving steadily northward, as if the heavens that bounded me could not contain so free a spirit, and something perhaps in the impulse of his wild heart which called him far away from the fields of men, and which found an answer in the heart of the boy who watched him till he vanished in the blue, and who had to stay on the farm while his soul was away to the wilderness,—all these sights and sounds and unknown longings had bound me fast to Waptonk the Wild, and made me resolve some day to follow him and find out what it was that called him northward when brooks were free and big woods budding and the spring impulse was in the heart of all living things.

Later Waptonk had called to me again from the same heavens; but now the arrowhead pointed southward, and the flight was altogether different. The lines of the wedge wavered and were often broken; it held closer to earth and was less certain in its magnificent onward rush; and the clear full-throated bugle-calls that had thrilled the boy's heart with their springtime clangor gave place to a curious communicative chatter, in which almost every note rose at the end to a falsetto. Now and then a strong, clear note, deeper and more peremptory, would sound at the head of the wedge, and instantly the wings would cackle an answer and swing into better line; but the cry had lost much of its joy and utter freedom, as the flight had lost its power and swift certainty.

I did not know then, in the autumn days, that these were mostly young birds which had never before followed the long trail; that at the head of every wedge was one of the old birds, pointing out the headlands by which they shaped their course; that the flight was less certain because the goslings had not yet reached their full power and must rest by the way; and that the cry was less stirring because spring no longer called them away by its throbbing love life and by the sweet home memories of quiet nesting places in the far Northland. Rather were they driven away from the things they loved; and now the security of the great, free, lonely wilderness must give place to constant watchfulness in a hostile land, where danger lurked and roared out upon them from every point and bay and feeding-ground. No wonder the flight wavered; no wonder the young voices rose to falsetto in amazement at the change from the quiet little pond, which had been all their world, to the vast panorama of seas and mountains and cities of men spread wide beneath their wings.

Then in the autumn days the boy, like all the rest of the male population in whom something of the old savage lingered under its coat of civilization, felt the hunter stir within him, and saw visions and dreamed dreams when the wild-goose call from the heavens came down to him as a kind of a challenge. When the weather was stormy and the flight was low, the boy would climb stealthily out of the rear window of the barn with the forbidden old musket close to his breast. Keeping the barn between his own line of flight and the kitchen windows, he would head across the brown fields to the woods, holding steadily and swiftly on his way to the little Widow Dunkle's, who kept an old gray goose. Sometimes he begged, sometimes he bribed, and sometimes, when the flight was irresistible and the widow away from home, he simply appropriated what he wanted with all his heart. There would be a rush among the fowls, squawking and quacking of hens and ducks, and one wild clarion yell from the old graylag goose as she found herself in chancery. Then the boy would scoot and dodge away to the big pond in the woods, with the old musket at trail and the old gray goose gripped tight under his elbow, *konk-konking* her resentment, but sensible enough, as all geese are when you take them right.

Next scene in the little comedy,—a boy hidden in the grass and bushes of a lonely point, scanning the heavens as if at any moment they might open and let wonders fall; and in front of him an old gray goose, with one foot anchored to a brick, swimming about and tip-tilting her tail to the skies as she splashed and probed the bottom for roots, gabbling to herself like a whole flock of geese in her wonder and delight at her strange surroundings. And when at last the wild geese came, and out of the sky came tumbling down the stirring clangor, how the centuries of domestic servitude fell away from the old graylag like a useless garment! Tugging at the stupid brick, with outstretched neck and quivering wings she recognized her own people and sent up a wild cry to call them down to share her loneliness—perhaps, who knows? to come and take her away with them. Then the boy,

hugging himself and holding his breath and loving the old goose supremely for her help, would lie still as a stone, only his eyes moving to follow the flight of the wild birds and see if they would come down to his bidding.

Generally the wedge kept steadily on, straight and true to its course; but every head was bent to bugle down an answer to the captive. Then the boy's heart was touched in turning away from the high flight to watch his old graylag. Beating her useless wings, struggling after her kindred as far as the anchor string would allow, she would call and call, and all the wildness of the lonely Northland was in her appealing summons. Long after the clangor had died away to a faint crackle and vanished in immeasurable distance, she would sit listening with neck upstretched, hearing, and in her heart answering, the call which had died away on the boy's less sympathetic ears.

After that there was no more joyous gabbling from Graylag. She would swim about silently, now pecking angrily at the restraining string, now raising her head to look and listen for her wild kindred, till twilight fell sadly on the pond and she would go home mute and passive under the boy's arm again.

One stormy day great luck headed towards the boy and made his heart jump at the thought of at last meeting the gray wanderers of the upper air that had so often set his heart a-longing. A great gang of wild geese, flying lower than usual, with the sides of their wedge broken by the sleet and irregular from weariness, passed near the pond on their southern migration. Their faint, confused honking roused all the wild longing in the heart of Old Graylag. Something too in their call, which she seemed to understand, made her sure they would come this time, and that she would know at last what the longing in her old heart meant. As she raised herself on her poor wings and sent out her clamorous appeal, the wild leader stopped, and the long wedge seemed to tumble together in a dense mass of cackle and confusion. Then the leader whirled; above the clamor came the deep honk of authority; the lines formed swiftly, with marvelous precision, and straight up the pond to the boy's hiding-place they came, a glorious big wedge of birds, honking, honking in joy at so good a resting-place, and nearly taking the heart out of Old Graylag as she clamored and tugged at her anchor and beat the water with her wings.

Then, all by himself, the boy saw a bit of Waptonk's drill school which old goose hunters on the coast have looked for many years in vain. High overhead they came till over the middle of the pond, when the leader whirled sharply to the right. The right-hand side of the wedge whirled after him, while the left wing halted and then turned in behind the leaders in a single long line. Every wing was now set stiffly; the clangor suddenly ceased, and

"When he winds down the invisible staircase of the winds"

down they came, round and around in a beautiful spiral, as if sliding down on an invisible winding staircase. Following the big leader came the long, magnificent line, which swung in a complete curve above him and half around the circle again; all with set wings and outstretched necks, gliding, wheeling, curving steadily downward in perfect order and perfect silence.

It was marvelous, the grace, the precision, the impressive silence of the stately procession down the spiral staircase of the winds, and the boy forgot the hunter in his intense wonder and admiration. One by one the great birds dropped their black webbed feet and slid gently along just over the surface for a brief moment, and then dropped with a quiet, restful splash into the water. An instant later they had swung together and a low, eager chatter began among them.

Now Old Graylag alone had been unimpressed by the wonderful descent, for other things were stirring wildly in her lonely heart. All the while they were coming down, so silent and stately, she kept up an hysterical cackle, with a wild beating of pinions and a frantic tugging at the anchor as she strove mightily to join her kindred. As they swung together with necks up suspiciously—for no wild water-fowl likes any welcome or demonstration beyond the universal uplifting of wings—she ceased her wild struggle and called softly. Instantly the leader answered and the whole flock drew in steadily towards the shore.

Behind the rough screen of grass and bushes the boy's heart began to beat loudly as he clutched his long musket. The hunter was wide-awake again, and here were the geese—great splendid birds that never before were nearer than the heavens—almost within gunshot, drawing steadily nearer and calling as they came on. In front of him the old gray goose, full of a nameless excitement, jabbered back at the flock and swung rapidly in small circles about her anchor. Her excitement increased; the flock halted, wavered, veered aside; then the heart of the old goose went after them in a wild *honk!* with a break in it like the fall of a tin pan. A tug, a plunge, a flurry of wings; the anchor string snapped and away she went, half flying, half running over the water, and plunged in among the wild birds in a smother of spray. In an instant she was swallowed up in a dense circle of gray backs and slender black necks with white cheek patches, and the whole flock drew swiftly away into open water, cackling and jabbering softly, with the nasal *konk-a-konk* of Old Graylag sounding incessantly above the hushed chatter of her wild kindred.

Late that day, after waiting long, cold hours in the vain hope that they would come near my hiding-place, I pushed out sadly in a leaky old tub of a boat to catch the Widow Dunkle's goose. The flock took alarm while I was yet far away; slanted heavily up-wind to the tree-tops, where with much calling and answering the young birds fell into line, and the wedge bore away swiftly seaward. After them went Old Graylag heartbroken, beating her heavy way over the water, calling and calling again to the flock that had now become only a confused tangle of wild voices over the treetops. Straight to the shore she went, and across a little wild meadow, still following the flock. When I caught her she was waddling bravely through the woods, stopping anon to call and listen; but she made no resistance when I tucked her under my elbow and carried her home and slipped her, unobserved in the darkness, into her accustomed place in the Widow Dunkle's duck coop.

That was the nearest I ever came, in boyhood days, to a close acquaintance with Waptonk the Wild; but always in the fall his voice roused the hunter as no other sound ever did; and always in the spring his clanging *jubilate* aroused the longing in the boy's heart to follow after him and find out what it was in the wild, lonely North that called him. Later, as a hunter, I grew acquainted with many of his winter ways, watched him feeding on the shoals or standing for sleep on the lonely sand bars, and thrilled to the rustling sweep of his broad wings as he swung in over my decoys.

The trained geese which were often used—descendants of sundry wing-tipped or wounded birds that had been saved to breed in captivity—were very different from Old Graylag. When the honk of wild geese was heard and the long wedge wavered over the pond, these trained birds would be loosed to circle far out from shore and with wild clamor call down their wilder kinsfolk. Then slowly, cautiously, as if they knew well the treacherous work they were doing, they would lead the wild birds in towards the blind till within range of the hidden gunners, when they would scatter suddenly and rush aside to get out of the way; and the decoyed and wondering geese would be left open to the murderous fire of the concealed hunters. An evil work, it seemed to me, in which I am glad to remember I took no part beyond that of watching with intense interest, and wondering at the cunning patience with which the old pot-hunter had trained his wild confederates.

Watching these trained decoys one day, it was hard to realize that the birds were but yesterday the wildest and wariest of all the feathered folk. Then the startling paradox occurred to me that the very wildest of the creatures are the easiest to tame by man and the quickest to adopt his ways. The sparrows that live about our houses all their days have little fear of men; but at the first attempt to catch them they are suspicious for life, and to domesticate them would be an impossibility. So with the ruffed grouse, a very tame bird in his native wilderness, that barely moves aside to let men pass; yet all attempts to domesticate him or to make him content with safe quarters and abundant fare have been, with a few rare exceptions, unaccountable failures. He lets you come near and watch him readily enough; but the moment you put him in your coop the very spirit of wildness takes possession of him, and he dies in the attempt to regain his freedom.

The wild goose, on the other hand, the wariest and wildest of birds when he comes among us in his migrations, giving wide berth to everything that has the least semblance to man or man's invention, and never letting you get within rifle-shot if his wary sentinels can detect your approach, will feed from your hand after he has been a few hours in your coop; and his descendants will take a permanent and contented place in your barn-yard. In the spring, when the migratory fever stirs within him, he will answer the clarion call of his fellows in the sky and spread wide his wings to join them; but that passes speedily, and he turns back to your dooryard and seems content even with the clipped wing which keeps him there while his brothers and kinsfolk fade away in the cold blue distance. Cases have been known in which a wounded goose, having been kept all winter, has flown away with a passing flock into the unknown North during the spring migration, and returned the next fall to the same barn-yard, bringing her brood with her. And so with the turkeys that range our fields; they are descendants of birds that but yesterday were ranging the woods as wild and unapproachable as wilderness ravens.

The first great lesson I learned in the years of following the wild goose as a hunter was one of tremendous respect for his wariness and intelligence. To call a person a goose would be an exaggerated

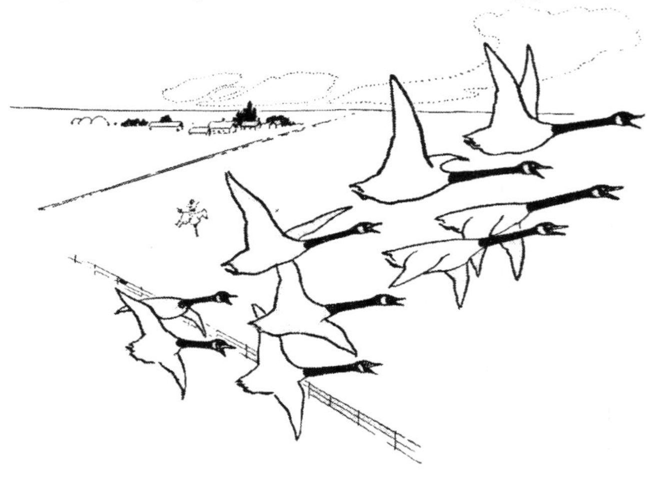

compliment, or a bit of pure flattery, if one but understood what he was saying. Wherever he feeds in the open, Waptonk has his sentinels posted on the highest point of observation—wise old birds that know their business—and it is next to impossible to approach a flock without being detected. Once it was enough to lead a cow slowly towards where the birds were feeding on the stubble and keep yourself hidden on the farther side of the grazing animal; but now Waptonk looks keenly under every cow to see if she have an extra pair of legs or no, and so other devices must be invented, only to be quickly fathomed by Waptonk's nimble wit, and then cast aside with the others as useless things. On the coast he still listens to the voice of his kind and comes to the trained decoys; and on the prairies a deep pit with wounded birds tied to stakes all about it and honking their fellows will sometimes bring him near enough for a quick shot. But these unfair advantages are in themselves a confession of man's failure; since by his own wit and aided by modern firearms he is no longer able to contend with the wit of a goose.

Elsewhere, especially in the great wheatfields of the Southwest, there is a humorous confession of man's impotence and Waptonk's superiority in the queer "goose cavalry,"—horsemen that go shooting and shouting about to frighten away from the growing wheat the thronging thousands of wild geese that cannot be circumvented or destroyed. And the most ridiculous thing in the whole proceeding is that the goose cavalryman must fume and fret under the thought that the exasperating birds understand him perfectly. They feed and gabble away serenely, paying no more serious heed to him than to any other scarecrow, until just before he gallops up, or foolishly tries to creep within range behind his horse, when the sentinel gives the alarm and the whole flock takes wing and settles down comfortably to feed in another part of the same wheat-field.

All this is the more remarkable in view of the fact that this marvelous shrewdness with which Waptonk evades the best inventions of men, far from being a matter of instinct, is imparted to him on the spot by his wise old leaders. For untold generations he has been born and bred in the waste places of the North, where he sees no man and where his life is singularly care-free and fearless. When he starts southward for the first time, full-grown and strong of wing, he knows absolutely nothing of the world of men. Left to himself and his own instincts he would speedily tumble into the first cunning pitfall, as his ancestors did when they met white man and his devices. Then old and young alike had little fear of man,—as they have little now in their wild northern home,—and met him with only the ordinary wild creature's watchfulness; but in a few seasons they learned better, and now the chief concern of the old birds on the southern migration is to keep the young well away from things that are dangerous. Fortunately for the young goose, his parents always lead the flock of which he is a part; and from them and from the old leaders, trained in the school of long experience, he speedily learns to shift for himself and to make his own way in a world of wits.

All these and many more things the boy learned as he followed Waptonk with the hunters; but still his chief question remained unanswered. From books and baymen alike, from explorers and the shrewd old pot-hunter of the Middleboro' ponds, he heard always the same story: how the honking wedge might be called down to decoys, and how the wary birds might be tolled or trapped or outwitted and killed; but what Waptonk was as a living creature, what thoughts were in his head and what feelings in his heart when he was far from men, in his own home where he could be himself,—that problem nobody answered. Something to be killed, rather than a living thing to be known and understood, was what met the boy at every turn and hushed his questions. And always in the spring, when the wild call of the wide voyagers floated down from the blue heavens, and the boy's eyes followed eagerly the rush of the great living wedge sweeping northward to love and liberty, something new and strange, yet familiar as the spring or the sunrise, stirred and awoke in the boy's heart and made him long to follow.

That is no strange experience, I think. Something stirs in the hearts of most men, and sweeps the years away and makes them boys again, with the impulse to wander and to do splendid things far away, when the first jubilant trumpet clangor of the wild goose comes down to them in the spring twilight. It was no surprise, therefore, but only the fulfilment of many years of quiet expectancy, when I crept out of the low spruces away up in the northern peninsula of Newfoundland, and found the end of my long quest. A subdued chatter of wild voices had called to me softly above the steady murmur of the river as I stole through the woods to the salmon pool in the early June morning. Following the sounds, which seemed very near at first, but which faded away like a will-o'-the-wisp when I tried to find them, they led me away from the river and out of the big woods to where an unknown barren lay just awake under the sunrise, greeting the intruder with the silent, questioning look of the wilderness. And there, close at hand in a little flashet, was Waptonk the Wild, waiting quietly as if he had always expected me.

Still and secret as my approach had been, with that curious unconscious effort to efface himself that marks the going of a man or an animal alone in the great wilderness, Waptonk had been watching me for some moments before I saw him. He was resting quietly in the middle of the flashet, a splendid big gander, with soft gray body that almost lost its outlines against the gray shore, and glossy black neck standing straight up from the water, and a pure white cravat rising on either side to his cheeks, like the immaculate "choker" of the old-fashioned New England minister. All the wildness and wariness seemed to have fallen away from him, as a man drops a useless garment when he enters his own home. He looked at me steadily, quietly, without fear; with a certain sense of dignity in every strong, graceful line of his body, and with an unmistakable sense of his responsibility in guarding that which was hidden away somewhere on the farther shore. My first wondering impression was, Can this be the same bird that I have followed so long in vain, whose name, in the expression "a wild-goose chase," is a symbol for all that is hopeless and inapproachable? There he sat, quiet, self-contained, without a tremor of fear or curiosity, and with no intention, so far as my eyes could discover, either to approach or to fly away.

I drew near quietly and sat down on the shore, while Waptonk swung easily back and forth on a short beat in front of me. As the minutes passed and I made no hostile sound or movement, the short patrol increased its swing till it covered an irregular half circle whose center was a point on the farther shore; and I knew then where I should find his nest and gray mate. Presently he began to talk,—a curious low gabble. Out of the grass and moss on the point rose a head and long dark neck to look at me steadily. Near it were low cheepings and whistlings, where the goslings had been hiding in silence till the danger passed by.

I rose at this, having found his secret, and made my way round the pond, with immense caution because of the quaking bogs and bottomless black mud that lurked under my feet at every step. Waptonk stopped his patrol to watch me a moment, then followed closely, keeping just abreast of me as I made my slow way along the treacherous shore. When I doubled the end of the little pond and drew near to where his nestlings were hidden, Waptonk turned to the shore and hurried to his mate ahead of me. A moment he stood over her reassuringly, bending to intertwine his neck with hers and to rub his cheek softly over her wings with a gesture that could mean only a caress. His head bent lower still to touch for an instant the goslings that were hiding in the moss; then he left them abruptly and rushed to where I was standing watching the amazing scene, and drew up defiantly, squarely across my path.

An involuntary thrill of admiration ran over me as I looked down at him standing there so strong and confident, ready to defend his own. "You splendid fellow; you brave knight, if ever there was one among the feathered folk!" I kept saying to myself. But I wanted to test him farther, and especially I wanted to see all that was hidden in the gray moss; so I started forward again cautiously.

At the first step a lightning transformation swept over Waptonk. Big as he was, he ruffled all his feathers and half spread his great wings till he looked twice his own size, and formidable enough to scare any prowler. Another step; then his eyes flashed, and lowering his head and black neck close to the ground he rushed straight at

" He rushed straight at me "

me, hissing like forty snakes, and with a gasping, terrifying cackle in his throat, as if his rage were choking him.

It was magnificent, this swift change from quiet dignity to raging defiance of an enemy ten times his size. The fierce hissing got into my nerves, spite of myself, and made me wonder if any wild animal, living constantly, as animals do, on the thin edge of flight and panic, could stand up against the terrifying sound for a moment. I remembered the time when, as a little boy, I had been soundly drubbed and beaten out of the barn-yard by an irate old gander, and watched now the great wings with a lively memory of what blows they could deal. Like a man caught in a fault, I had absolutely no defense; for Waptonk was on his own ground, and I had no business whatever in meddling with his affairs. To throw myself upon him, therefore, and by brute force to overcome the noble fellow defending his little ones, was out of the question; as plainly impossible as to rob a bird's nest or to beat a child. But suppose Noel, my big Indian, should chance that way on his perpetual quest for new beaver ground? I could see the queer squint in his eye and the grin on his wrinkled face as he watched me hopping over the bogs, with the old gander nipping at my heels and spanking me with his broad wings as he chased me gloriously out of his bailiwick. That was too much, even for the sake of encouraging Waptonk as he deserved; so instead of

running away I sank down quietly in the moss, waiting half humorously to take my medicine and fully expecting to get it "good and plenty."

Quite near me he stopped, his head down close to the ground, his tongue bent up like a spring into the roof of his mouth, hissing vigorously and watching me keenly out of his bright eyes to see the effect of his demonstration. It flashed upon me instantly why he bristled his feathers and raised his wings, while he carried his neck and head down close to the ground, like a big snake. The wings, his only weapons, were half raised for a blow; but the fierce-hissing yet harmless head would surely hold the attention of any attacking animal—just as an owl snaps his beak to frighten you and keep your eyes away from his dangerous claws until he gets them into you unexpectedly. Any wild animal, if he were brave enough to attack, would naturally avoid the snakelike hissing and leap over it for the larger body, only to be met by a stinging blow in the face from the powerful wings. If the delicate neck were carried high, any animal would naturally leap for it, and Waptonk's fight would be over almost before he could strike a blow. As it is, Waptonk carries his most vulnerable point as close to the ground as possible, as a ship carries her magazine below the water-line, and by scaring an animal with his snakelike hiss he gets a fair chance to use his weapons, and so takes care of himself splendidly against all prowlers.

Waptonk was evidently amazed at my quiet. Having expected either fight or flight, he was thrown off his balance and hardly knew how to meet the emergency. I fancied I could see it all in his eyes as he looked at me steadily. A moment or two he kept his defensive attitude, till the hissing gradually died away. He raised himself suddenly and threshed his great wings in my face. I could feel the strong wind of them on my cheek and measure the nervous muscular beat under his feathers as he tried their power. Then he put his head down to the ground and hissed again, daring me to come on.

Ten yards behind him sat his mate, her head raised out of the grass, watching us steadily without a sound. Suddenly she uttered a low call with a curious accent of warning and reassurance. It was a communication to her champion, plainly enough, for he wavered slightly for the first time from his intense attitude. The next moment she slipped out of the grass into the pond, and after her came five goslings,

alert little bundles of yellow-brown fuzz, that walked steadily across the shore, with a funny effect of carrying their knees up close to their shoulders, and glided easily into the friendly waters. There was another low call from the gray mate; then Waptonk, though he had not turned his head nor taken his keen eyes for an instant from my face, turned swiftly aside and threw himself into the water. A push or two from his powerful webs, and he was floating safely far beyond my reach, still looking back at me alertly over his shoulder as he surged away.

The little family glided swiftly along the pond shore, the mother leading them and talking to them reassuringly. Between them and me hovered Waptonk, swinging back and forth on his watchful patrol, till they disappeared from sight; then he glided silently after them into a muddy lagoon where the treacherous bogs forbade any human to follow.

An hour later the little wild family stole shyly out of the haven where they had hidden, and found me sitting quietly just where I had first appeared. If they were surprised or uneasy, they gave no sign of their feelings beyond a bright, inquisitive look, but swam slowly past me and climbed the bank where it was worn hard by their feet, and started across the barren on their day's foraging. For hours I followed them, keeping out of sight as much as possible, watching with keenest interest their feeding and discipline, and noting especially the crude beginnings of that wedge formation with which they would later make their first long flight southward ahead of the autumn gales.

Wherever they went, Waptonk, the big gander, was near them, hovering on the outskirts, or watching over them keenly from every little hillock that commanded a wider view of the great barren. He ate but little, and apparently only incidentally. His whole business seemed to be to guard his little flock while the mother led them about to feed, or trained them to the perfect discipline that is the wonder of all those who have ever watched wild geese. And when at midday the feeding was done, and the goslings were sunning themselves on the bank of another flashet under the mother's eye, Waptonk took wing and bore away swiftly over the woods and marshes to the ocean; as if in his cramped life he wanted room and exercise, or perhaps just a glimpse of the wide sea, which he loved, as all others do who have once felt the spell of its boundless mystery. For within the hour he was back again, as usual, standing guard over his own.

Later, as I returned day after day to watch the gray voyagers that had so long attracted me, I saw a rare bit of Waptonk's care and sagacity. One of the goslings, more headstrong than the others, in wandering away from the leader over a treacherous bit of bog-land found himself stogged in some soft mud that he attempted to cross too hurriedly and carelessly. He floundered desperately for a moment, called sharply, and then lay perfectly quiet with wings extended on the mud to keep himself from sinking deeper. Instantly the mother bird called all the young close about her, raised her neck high to look over them at her helpless gosling, then turned her head and honked deeply to the gander. Waptonk had already seen the danger from his point of vantage and rose heavily in the air. Circling once with bent head over the little fellow in the mud, as if to understand the situation, he turned and flapped over him, reaching down to seize a wing

in his bill. So, with the youngster kicking vigorously and flapping his free wing to help himself, he half dragged and half carried his careless offspring over the mud, and hiked him out upon the moss with a final unnecessary jerk that seemed to tell him roughly to take better care of himself another time. But he lowered his head to rub his cheek softly down the little fellow's neck and over his wings, again and again, before he walked quietly away to his post as if nothing whatever had happened.

Then came the final scene, which made me tingle in my hiding, increasing the strong desire that rarely leaves me to understand what passes in the heads and hearts of the Wood Folk. The mother went to the careless one and brought him back to where the flock were waiting. Then standing in the midst of her brood she seemed to be talking to them, first in a low chatter, then in a strange silent communication, in which not a muscle moved, but in which every neck was raised in the attitude of tense attention. A moment later the flock was moving across the barren, cheeping, whistling, feeding as before.

Late in the afternoon, as I watched by the home flashet, there was another scene altogether different; and here were many things that a man could not be expected to understand, though I saw and admired them often enough. As the sun sank and the pointed shadows of the spruces came creeping out across the barren, the little flock came wandering back, as is the custom with wild geese, to spend the night by the nest where they were born, and to sleep contentedly under their mother's wings, while the old gander kept watch and ward in the darkness. For Waptonk is more of a land bird than any of the ducks. The forward set of his legs shows that Nature intended him to walk as well as swim; and he will never sleep in the water if he can find a safe and quiet spot to rest on the shore.

At sight of the familiar place the little family that I had watched all day long suddenly stopped their hungry wandering and came running in a close group, heads all up and whistling, to tumble down the slope and throw themselves with glad splashes into the friendly water, which was all aglow now with the splendors of the sunset. There they drank and washed themselves, and played together in little races and scuffles, and,stopped their play to stretch their necks down to the oozy bottom for roots that they had overlooked, or for earth and pebbles to aid their digestion. Then as the shadows lengthened they glided to an open spot on the bank to preen and gabble softly; while the big parent birds, their own preening finished as they watched the play of their little ones, went from one to another, rubbing them tenderly with their white cheeks, chattering over each one in turn, and in twenty little indescribable ways showing their fondness—their gladness also that the long good day was done and they were safe at home once more.

Perhaps this was all imagination; but, even so, a man must look in his heart, not in the psychologies or natural histories, if he would understand half of what the Wood Folk are doing. Here before my eyes was a little family that had come back in the sunset, after much wandering and some danger, to the one spot in the great wilderness that they knew well, where life began for the goslings, and where each familiar thing seemed to welcome them and make them feel at home. Over them stood the parents, strong and watchful against the world, but bending their necks tenderly to tell their little ones by the soft caress of their cheeks that they loved and understood them. A low, contented gabble filled the twilight stillness, unintelligible perhaps, yet telling plainly by its changing accents the goslings' changing feelings from the day's bright excitement to the evening's sleepy content, and recalling to me in a sudden wave of tenderness the chatter of a little child far away in

the same twilight, who could speak no words as yet, but whose feelings I could understand perfectly as she talked back to the friendly universe and then crooned herself and her dolly to sleep, alone in her own little crib. A great tide of light rolled suddenly over the plain from the west as the clouds lifted, bathing all things in a rosy splendor, and the young birds stopped their chatter to turn their heads and watch silently for a moment as the glory swept over them; and the voices were different, more hushed and sleepy, yet with a slight note of wonder, like birds wakened by a light, when I heard them again. In the nearest thickets a choir of thrushes were ringing the Angelus; nearer a solitary vesper-sparrow, hidden in the gray moss, was singing his hymn to the evening; an unknown call floated down from the distant hills; a fox barked in answer; while the river hushed its roar as the night fell and went singing down on its way to the sea. And to all these sounds, and to every wave of light and passing shadow and restless wing of the eddying plovers, the young birds responded instantly with low cheeps and whistles, drawing nearer and nearer together to feel a last touch of their parents' white cheeks; while I lay and watched them, myself drifting away into that delicious border-land of feeling and sense-impression in which the young birds live so constantly, where all conscious thought vanishes and one becomes alive in every nerve and finger-tip to the sights and sounds and subtle harmonies of the world. For Nature reveals not only herself, but some beautiful and forgotten part of a man's own soul, when she finds him responsive in the wilderness.

Slowly the glory deepened and faded, and the crimson flush that had spread wide over the great barren came creeping back into the west out of which it had come. After it came the silence, hushing the goslings' chatter and the birds' hymn; and only the river was left singing to itself through the listening woods. Over the vast plain came again the sea-wind swinging its fragrant censer, from which fell now only heavy and drowsy odors; and the fleecy mists that I had seen rise at dawn settled softly again to cover the sleeping earth like a garment. I could no longer see the birds that I had followed all the long, sunny day; but where the little family stood a soft gray shadow blurred the open shore; and from it came now and then a sleepy, inquisitive peep as some little one stirred uneasily, and then a deep, quiet answer to tell him that all was well, and that he was not alone in the darkness.

That was my first real meeting with Waptonk, my first answer to the question which had always been in my heart, and which neither the books nor the hunters could answer, as to what he was like in his own land, where the guns and decoys of men might not enter. And I was satisfied, perfectly satisfied, as I turned away in the twilight across the wild barren to where my little tent by the salmon river was waiting.

PEQUAM
THE FISHER

PEQUAM THE FISHER

PEQUAM the fisher, the Cunning One as Simmo calls him, who follows your snow-shoe track but never crosses it, is one of the shadows of the big woods. A dark shadow indeed to the Wood Folk, for wherever he goes death follows close behind him; and a shadow to your eyes also, for when you do see him, unexpectedly, after much watching and patience, he darts up the hillside, leaping and dodging, vanishing and appearing and vanishing again, like one of the shadows that the sunbeams are chasing when a brisk wind drives the clouds away and the woods are filled with rustlings and uncertainties.

Why is he called the fisher? That is one of the mysteries. Ask the half-breeds of the great Barren Grounds, and they may tell you, perhaps, that he is called fisher because he is a most industrious thief in stealing the fish with which they bait their traps, in angling them out of the cunning devices without getting his own paw caught or bringing the heavy deadfall down on his own back. The name Weejack, however, which still clings to him there, has no thought of fish or fishing in it, but suggests rather the elves and goblins, the cunning and mischievous Little Folk, that are supposed to haunt the solitudes and play havoc with the trapper's saple line.

The earlier naturalists, catching rare glimpses of Pequam and trusting to their own knowledge rather than to the Indians' better understanding, probably called him fisher because they confused him with Keeonekh the otter, whom he slightly resembles and who is a famous fisherman. Like all weasels—and next to Carcajou the wolverine he is greatest and fiercest of his tribe—he likes fish; but I have never known him to catch one unaided save once; and then he leaped into a shallow pool among the rocks,where the receding waters had left a big salmon half stranded, and darted about like a fury in a blinding smother of water till he gripped his slippery prize securely and dragged him away into the shadows.

Pequam has other names. Black Fox he is called in places where he is but rarely seen, though he bears no relation to the black or silver fox, and Pennant's Marten by the bookish people, and Black Cat by all the Maine trappers, who follow him on the spring snows when he is gorged with food, and who catch him cunningly at last asleep in a hollow log—and that is the only way I have ever tried in which I have really caught a weasel asleep. But whatever his name, Pequam has the same nature wherever I have found or heard of him; whether on the high mountain ranges, or the bleak Labrador barrens, or the silent shadow-filled northern woods, —a crafty, restless, bloodthirsty haunter of every trail, even of your own; at once shy and daring, springing in tense alarm at the slightest unknown squeak or chirp or rustle, yet with a screeching ferocity at times, when you corner him, that makes your spine tingle.

Because he is little known, even to the naturalists, let me

describe him just as you meet him at home in the woods. If you see him at all, which is not likely unless you follow him for miles on the snow and find his kill and then track him to his den, you will be conscious chiefly of a black streak drawn swiftly up the hillside and vanishing over the top of a rock or a mossy log. If you get any idea of the creature at all, it will be something like that of an enormous black cat with a terrier in swift pursuit. If he but stand for an instant to see what frightened him and give you one of the rarest sights in the woods, you will see an exceedingly nervous animal, suggesting at once a cat and a huge weasel. He is much larger than a house cat, with short legs and a pointed face, like a marten's, and glossy black fur. That is as far as you will ever get in your description; except perhaps the tail, which, you see, is long and soft and glossy as he vanishes over the log. And, like a scared cat, he fluffs it out like a bottle-brush to make it look big and to scare you should you attempt to follow him.

Two or three times in the woods I have had just such glimpses of Pequam as I have described; but, except in hunting on the snow, only once have I seen him plainly when he had no idea I was watching him. I was sitting quietly in the woods at daybreak, watching for deer and moose on Matagammon, when there was a rustle behind me and Moktaques went hopping by in the crazy, erratic way that hares have when hunted. " Kagax is after him," I thought, and turned to watch for the weasel, at the same time picking up a stick to stop the bloodthirsty little wretch's hunting. Then out of the underbrush darted Pequam, his muzzle twitching, tail quivering,—darting, leaping, dodging, halting, all on fire with excitement. Every hair on his body seemed to be alive and filled with nerves; and I thought instantly of a young fisher that I used to watch for hours at a time in his cage. Whether sleeping or waking, on the ground or in his tree, he seemed to have eyes, ears, and senses all over him. A squeak, a chirp, a scratch,—the slightest sound, and instantly he leaped from what he was doing and twisted his head and whirled and leaped again. Once when he was apparently sound asleep I brought my thumb and finger nails together and snapped the edges. A sound so faint would hardly trouble the dreams of even a sleeping wolf; but on the instant Pequam had leaped to his feet wide-awake and was wrinkling his nose in my direction.

Just this same impression of intense vitality and alertness swept over me now as the wild creature passed before me, fairly quivering from nose to tail tip. Not ten feet from my hand, where the hare had made a wild jump, he stopped for an instant, twisted his head in a half circle to catch the scent, darted forward, ran back again with his nose to the ground; and then, finding he was off scent and running a back track, instead of turning, as any other animal would have done, he simply leaped, whirled in the air like a flash, and came down in his tracks facing in the opposite direction. It was the quickest, the most

"He had picked up the trail and darted away"

intense action I have ever seen in a living animal; and yet it was probably just an ordinary movement in Pequam's daily life. An instant later he had picked up the trail and darted away, absolutely unconscious that I had watched him.

As a hunter Pequam has no equal among the Wood Folk. He follows a trail with all the persistency of a weasel, and he darts forward with marvelous quickness when his nose has brought him within striking distance of his game. Of a score of fisher trails that I have followed in the winter woods, never a one but brought me sooner or later to the scene of his killing, with its record written as plainly as if the eye had seen it all. You may follow the track of Eleemos the fox, the Sly One as Simmo calls him, for days at a time, and find only that he has caught nothing and has lain down to sleep far more hungry than you are yourself. Or you may trace the round, deep pugs of Upweekis the lynx for uncounted miles through the bare, white, empty woods, and get at last a kind of sympathy for the big, savage, stupid fellow as you think how ravenous he must be; for the tracks lead to nothing but disappointments, at the beaver house, at the rabbit's form, beside the deer yard, and at the hole in the snow where the grouse plunged for the night. But follow Pequam a little way and you come speedily to the story of good hunting: here a mouse, and there a hare, and there a squirrel, and there a deer. Careful, now ! He is gorged and sleepy; and you will find him, not far away, asleep in a hollow tree under the snow.

Spite of his size Pequam climbs and moves among the big trees with all the sureness and agility of a squirrel, traveling long distances overhead, and even following his game by leaping from branch to branch. Like the squirrel he can jump down from an enormous height, flattening his body and tail against the air so as to break his fall, striking the ground lightly and darting away as if he enjoyed the dizzy plunge. And, like the larger cats, he sometimes creeps over his game on a lofty limb and leaps down upon it like a thunderbolt; though, unlike Pekompf the wildcat and Lhoks the panther, I have never known him to watch in a tree over the runways. His nose is too good and his patience too poor to lead him to these pot-hunting and abominable methods.

It is in following Pequam's trail through the snow that you learn, as you do with most large animals, the story of his life. For the northern forests, in winter especially, seem but bare and tenantless places. Far in the South life seems to be the order of the universe : earth, air, and water swarm at all times with a multitude of creatures. Here all is different. Silence and death seem to have gripped the world and emptied it. From early

morning, when the intense cold silences all things, to the short midday, when the feeble sun brings forth a jay's cry or a squirrel's disturbing chatter, and on to the early twilight, when the trees groan again and crack like pistols as the frost snaps the tightening bark, you glide along silently and alone on your snow-shoes; and save for the crossbills and chickadees and the rolling tattoo of the log-cock you seem utterly alone in the universe. No broad wing or gloss of fur or gray shadow of a deer disturbs the sharp outlines of the still tree bolls on every hand. Your own breath, as it drifts away in a cloud of frost among the trees, is the only sign of a living animal in all the snowy landscape.

Now look down at your feet. You are standing where the dainty trail of a fox crosses the broad lead of a porcupine and follows it a little way doubtfully. Eleemos is uncertain, you see, whether to turn aside or go on; debating with his shrunken stomach whether or not he is hungry enough to risk being struck through with cruel barbs for a coarse mouthful; undecided whether to follow Unk Wunk and perhaps find him safe rust again to luck and for a sweeter mouthful to ween a poor fox and death. There ! he follows the trail; and by that you may know he is more than hungry.

Life is here, you see; though it is now hidden away where it takes more than eyes to find it. Tracks are everywhere, all kinds of tracks, telling their stories of last night's wanderings, from the dainty tracery of the wood-mice to the half-filled path that leads you to the moose-yard on the other side of the great ridge. Follow any of them and you find life, or the plain record of life, that goes swiftly and silently to its chief end and concerns itself diligently about its own business. There, a little farther on, are your own snow-shoe slots of yesterday. And see, close beside them, following every turn and winding of your trail but never crossing it, are the cunning tracks of Pequam the fisher. Clear to your camp in a five-mile circle he followed your trail, and even now, behind you, he may be sniffing again at the new, strange tracks that rouse his curiosity.

Once, feeling that I was followed, I stole back cautiously and caught him hanging to my heels like a shadow; but why he follows my trail I have never been able to find out. It is a good plan, in the winter woods, to scatter food along your trail, for it overcomes the Wood Folk's distrust of man's footprints; but long before I found that out and practiced it Pequam had followed me. Perhaps he

has followed the trappers so long, to steal the bait from their marten traps, that it has become a habit.

It was on a morning like this, still and cold and lifeless, that I left the big lumber camp on the Dungarvon and struck off eastward for the barrens. I was after caribou; but two miles away in the woods I ran across old Newell the Indian, whose hunting camp was far up the river, moving swiftly along, with his eyes on a fresh trail.

"Hello, brother! what you hunt um?" I hailed him.

For answer he pointed with a grunt to the snow, where a fisher had gone along that morning as if some one were after him.

" Pequam in a hurry this morning. Thinks if Newell around, fisher better mog along somewhere else," I ventured; and the grim old face before me softened at the tribute to his skill in hunting.

" Oh, I get um," he said, smiling. " Das de fellow rob my saple traps. Find um where he kill deer dis morny. Now he go off wid hees belly full, sleepy, oh, sleepy. Find um bimeby, pretty soon quick now. You wan' go along help um ? " he added invitingly.

That was a new kind of hunting for me; so I left the caribou gladly and followed the old Indian. He had no gun; only an ax; and I was curious to know how he intended to catch so spry and wary an animal unaided; but I asked no questions, following silently and keeping out to one side of the trail, looking far ahead for a glimpse and a possible shot at Pequam among the trees. Indeed, it was probably the sight of my rifle and a light ax at my belt that caused Newell to issue his invitation.

The fisher was plainly suspicious or alarmed, for he was traveling with marvelous craftiness. Newell assured me that Pequam had neither nor smelled him. Probably he had eaten full and was now minded to lie down for a long sleep, and, like a bear seeking a winter den after the telltale snow has fallen, was making a cunning trail to deceive and mislead any that might try to find him. This was my own explanation and good enough for the moment; but later Newell gave a very different reason for the crooked trail we were following.

Again and again the trail doubled on itself where Pequam came back for a distance, stepping in his own footprints, and then leaped away in a great side jump into some thick cover where his new tracks were hidden. Newell, who was watching for such things, generally saw the trick and turned aside; but more than once he was deceived, and we went on to find the trail ending abruptly with a single footprint in the snow. Then we would turn back and hunt on either side till we picked up the trail again.

Twice the tracks ended at the foot of a great tree where Pequam had climbed and ran among the branches overhead; and then we had to circle widely to find where he had leaped down and run on again. Once he tunneled for a long distance under the snow; and when we found the trail it was far out to one side and running at right angles to his former course. So we followed him, mile after mile, and I had long given up the thought of shooting in the fascination of working out the riddle which Pequam had spread for us, when Newell, who had been growing more and more cautious for the past ten minutes, stopped suddenly and pointed ahead. And when I glided up to him there was no sign of a den or a hidden log, but only a little hollow half filled with a flurry of snow where the trail disappeared, as if Pequam had suddenly taken wings to himself and flown away.

" Where is he ? " I whispered.

" Oh, we got um now, good place," chuckled Newell. " Pequam tink he fool um ol' Injun; hide hees footin'. Now he tink safe, go sleep. Guess he fool self dis time—By cosh ! oh, by cosh ! "

From a great hole in the top of a fallen log, fifty feet away, a black streak shot out and vanished in a flurry of snow. Pequam, instead of going in at this hole, had tunneled out of sight for ten or fifteen feet and had gone in at the opposite end of the log, which was hidden by the deep snow and bending evergreens. A cunning trick; for any one approaching the half-buried log would see the inviting hole at the top but find no track leading up to' it, and so would conclude naturally that the den was unoccupied. Had we been an hour later we would have found him heavy with sleep in the log; but we had followed too hot on his trail. He had barely settled himself down in his warm den under the snow when our approach startled him and he was off on another crooked trail.

We stopped where we were to "bile kittle"; for the cold of the northern forests is killing in its intensity, and the moment you cease action that moment Nature clamors for fire and food with an insistence never known elsewhere. Late in the afternoon, after following the fresh trail through all its doublings and windings, we came to where it leaped aside without warning into a dense thicket of low firs. There it ended, as if the ground had opened to swallow Pequam; but just beyond a long mound showed where a fallen log lay buried under the snow, and we knew we should find him there fast asleep.

Unslipping the light ax, I moved cautiously to the smaller end of the log, while Newell crouched at the butt and began to shovel aside the snow with a snow-shoe. My end of the log was solid; in the whole shell after I had laid it bare of snow I found only a single hole, and that hardly big enough to admit a squirrel. Meanwhile Newell had pushed a pole into the hollow butt till it was seized savagely and almost jerked out of his hand. A fierce snarl and a muffled scratching told us plainly that we had reached at last the end of the trail.

Very deliberately the old Indian cut a dozen more poles, while I stood guard, and wedged them tightly in the hollow butt. Next he enlarged the squirrel hole, and I had a glimpse of glossy fur as Pequam rushed back toward the place where he had entered, only to find it shut securely. The squirrel hole was then closed by stakes driven through to the rotten wood beneath, and Pequam was caught, with only some six feet of hollow shell to rage around in.

I confess I would gladly enough have stopped here; for the sight of any trapped animal, however fierce, that has known all its life only absolute liberty, always awakens in me the desire to break its bars and set it free again. But Newell had no such scruples. Here was a prime fur worth eight dollars, to say nothing of plundered marten traps. The fire that sleeps in an Indian's eyes and that always kindles at the sight of game began to flash as he chopped a long notch through the top of the shell, driving in stakes as he advanced, and slowly but surely pinning Pequam into a space where a blow of the ax would finish it all.

Through the narrow slit I could see him, the flash of his eye and the white gleam of his teeth under his brown muzzle as he tried the opening, and then the sweep of his bushy tail as the ax drove him aside. Again and again he whirled on us savagely; for, unlike the fox and bear that know when you have won and that lie down quietly for the blow, Pequam rights and defies you to the very end. Game killer and robber of traps he may be; but traps are barbarous things at best, and the animal that robs them is only saving some innocent life from suffering, though he knows it not. Here he was, the shadow of the woods become solid substance at last, his marvelous cunning overmatched by man's intelligence. Not a chance left in the tough shell that held him fast, while the steel bit nearer and nearer and the stakes pinned him in. And there was something magnificent, an appeal not to be answered lightly, in the way he clung to life, claimed it, fought for it, and screeched out at us defiantly that his life was his own and we must not take it away.

" Got um safe now," I ventured at last.

"Safe!" grunted the Indian between the steady *chucks* of his ax, "by cosh, Pequam never safe till he dead; an' den he fool me two, tree time wen he only play dead. Bes' cock um dat gun; Pequam got plenty tricks he ant try yet." But there was no need of the gun, and I did not look to see the end. Before the short twilight had fallen on the woods we had stroked the splendid fur and valued it, and were heading swiftly for the little hunting camp on the river with Pequam's black coat hanging limp and soft and warm between the Indian's shoulders.

THE TRAIL OF THE CUNNING ONE

THE TRAIL OF THE CUNNING ONE

THAT night, in the queer little hunting camp by the river, while the birch logs glowed on the stone hearth and sang for the last time the songs which the winds had taught them, old Newell answered my questions about the fisher we had caught, and told me of his lonely trapper's life and the many trails he had followed. Under his skillful hands as he worked, Pequam's glossy skin changed its face and crept down to the very end of the long cedar stretcher, ready at last to take its place in the row of marten and fox and otter pelts that hung outside, touched and made fragrant by the wood smoke, and turning, turning for the last breath of the forest wind that stole in through the sides of the little *commoosie*.

What puzzled and interested me most was the Indian's confident declaration that Pequam had neither seen nor winded him that morning, but had simply felt the presence of an enemy on his trail, and so had taken to doubling and traveling among the branches in order to throw him off the track.

"Now I tell you now," he said earnestly, in answer to my suggestion that it was merely a precautionary measure, such as the bear takes before denning for the winter, " Pequam, jus' same all animals, know good many ting widout knowin' how he know. So long you jus' watch urn animal, he don't fraid 't all. Don't see, don't hear, don't smell; ev'thing jus' right; go on feedin', playin'; feel good inside. Now you go get you gun, follow hees footin'. Bimeby he stop; wag hees ears; sniff, sniff; look all round de hwoods. Don't hear, don't see, don't smell noting; get fraid an' run 'way jus' same. Plenty black cat in clese h woods. You follow an' find out for youself."

It was the old question that one runs up against everywhere in the woods, in his own hunting and in the experience of woodsmen, the unknown sixth sense, or feeling of danger, which sometimes warns a creature beyond the reach of any known sense, and which seems to imply a kind of silent mental communication among animals. Several times since then I have followed Pequam's trail and learned something about his hunting, and in every case have found much to justify the Indian's conclusion. When Pequam kills a large animal and gorges himself, he goes but a mile or two —often much less than that—and hides him away to sleep, making but slight effort to confuse his trail. Follow it now quietly, and you see where it disappears in the snow; and somewhere just beyond you will find Pequam asleep in a hollow log. But if you find the fresh track where he returns to his kill and follow it swiftly before he has settled down to sleep, he begins doubling and tunneling and traveling overhead long before it would seem possible that any sight or sound or smell of you could drift away over the hills to where the Cunning One is hiding his trail from the telltale snow.

Once, while following a fresh track, old Newell had a curious experience of Pequam's cunning; and last summer, when I noticed a fisher's track on the shore of Grassy Pond, under K'tahdin, my guide told me unasked of a similar occurrence which he had himself witnessed last spring when he was trapping among the Sourdnahunk Mountains. Newell found where Pequam had killed a deer on the crust, and followed the trail through the soft snow that had fallen over night, not half an hour after the fisher had left it. Mile after mile he swept along on his snow-shoes, through the swamps and over the hills, pushing the fisher hard and unwinding swiftly every turn and double and side jump and tunnel in the cunning trail. Pequam was heavy and tired. Two or three times Newell saw him plainly, but with his old gun, whose lock he must protect from the snow, he was not quick enough for a shot; and still the game held on, and at every turn laid some new snarl or puzzle for the old Indian's eyes to unravel. Late in the afternoon the trail turned abruptly from the ridge, which it had been following for miles, and headed straight and swift for a cedar swamp.

There were plenty of deer here. The spring hunger had driven them out of their yards; and in the early morning or late afternoon, when the crust hardened enough to bear their weight, they could get at the cedar boughs, which till then had been too high to reach. So long as they spread their legs or went softly, the crust would bear them up; but at the first heavy plunge they sank through to their shoulders, and were almost helpless.

Half-way through the swamp the hunted fisher winded a large deer and leaped straight at him. The tracks showed that it was not his usual crafty hunting, but a straight, swift drive, with probably a savage snarl to add to the terror of his rush. At the first startled bound Hetokh the buck sank to his withers. A dozen more plunges, and he lay helpless. Pequam raced alongside, leaped for his throat, and gave the death wound. He watched for a moment, crouching in the snow, till the buck lay still; then he ran on again without stopping to eat or drink. Newell, far behind, puzzling out the trail, neither saw nor heard anything of the swift tragedy, but read it all from the snow a half-hour later.

Straight back to the hills went Pequam, leisurely, carelessly now, and without making the slightest effort to hide his trail, as he had done all day, crept into the first good hollow log and lay down to sleep. Newell found him there and wedged him in without trouble, and took his skin within sight of the spot where the deer lay stiffening in the snow.

Now the curious thing about the killing is this, that Pequam was running for his life, with no time to lose or to throw away. He had already killed one deer and had eaten more than he wanted, and, with an enemy after him, would disgorge some of what he already carried rather than take more to make him heavy. Indeed, after a kill and a full meal, Pequam, when no enemy is near, usually lies quiet for days at a time, drowsing away in his hollow log. A certain blind ferocity might perhaps account for his killing the deer; but that leaves his subsequent carelessness unaccounted for. And besides, unlike their smaller and more bloodthirsty kinsman the weasel, neither fisher nor marten seem to kill for the lust of killing. They kill only when hungry, and usually go back to any large game until it is eaten up to the very bones before they hunt or kill again.

All this passed through my mind rapidly, and the Indian, in answer to my inquiries, confirmed my idea of the fisher's ordinary habits. Then I put the final question:

"Why on earth, then, did Pequam kill another deer? "

"Wy he kill um dat tother deer? Cause he tink Injun hongry, das wy he kill um." And then, as my eyes questioned his in the firelight, " Wy, you spose now, Pequam follow trail heself, jus' same I follow heem all day, huh ? Cause he hongry; cause he want meat. Das wy black cat, das wy hwolf, das wy all animal follow trail all day long in snow. He hongry; he want meat. Bimeby—*roofh! scritch !* kill urn deer. Eat um plenty; lie down sleep; don' follow trail no more."

" Now I follow Pequam," continued Newell earnestly, " jus' same he follow deer. Pequam hide, run, climb tree, go under snow; try fool um Injun. All time Injun keep right on; thoo cedar swamp, up big hill, down tother side,—ev'where Pequam go, Injun follow hees footin'. Bimeby Pequam tink: 'Injun hongry; Injun want meat; Injun want eat um me.' Den he go kill um deer. Tink, p'raps, Injun eat plenty meat; go 'way; don' follow hees trail no more."

Startling as was the explanation, there was a grain of reason in it, and I give it because I have none other to offer. Years later, when I asked the Maine guide how he accounted for his fisher's action, he gave precisely the same reason, though more than ten years and two countries and many hundreds of miles separated the two occurrences. The black cat, he said, must have thought or felt in his own dumb way that by killing a deer and leaving it there untouched he might satisfy and turn aside the enemy that followed on his trail. In no other way could he account for the subsequent carelessness with which the fisher left the game untouched and lay down to sleep in the first good den. For Pequam, spite of his cunning, has room in his head for only one idea at a time; and so long as you let him keep that idea, you may plan safely to catch him.

A curious instance of this came out a few days later, when I took up my abode with the Indian and went with him to the traps, or wandered alone through the woods following the crooked trails. Newell had a long line of marten traps —saple line, he called it—following a ridge for nearly ten miles crossing the river and returning on the other side. And down at the lower end was a rough log cabin where we could find shelter if overtaken by night or a sudden storm.

The traps, which were scattered at intervals along the ridges, were little pens made of stakes or slabs or stones. Inside the pen was a bait of fish or flesh; and over the narrow entrance slanted a weighted log resting on a trigger, so arranged that when an animal entered and seized the bait the deadfall came down promptly and broke his back. As he visited the traps Newell frequently carried a *drag*, a couple of flayed muskrats tied to a string, which he dragged along behind him, making a scented trail from one trap to another. Any marten crossing this trail would

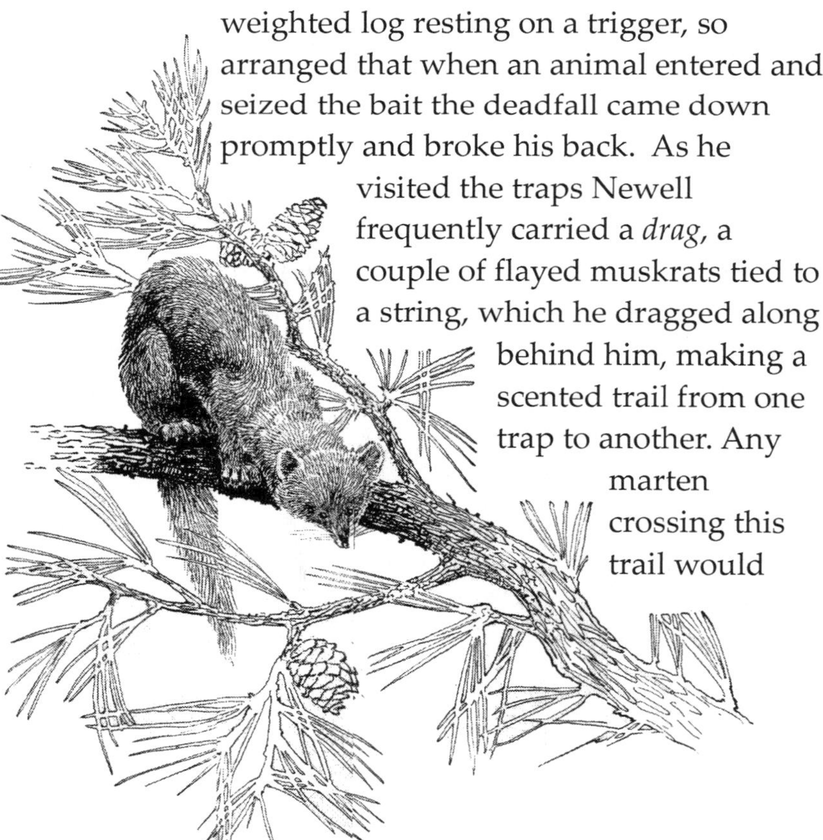

turn and follow it, and so come straight to one of the traps.

One day a large fisher struck the line and made havoc of it. Pequam either tore the pen to pieces, or else he entered it craftily from the rear and sprung the deadfall harmlessly, and then ate the bait at his leisure. A dozen traps were so destroyed, and one valuable marten which had been caught was eaten with the bait. For nearly a month this had continued. Hardly a day but Pequam found the line somewhere, destroying traps and good marten skins until his hunger was satisfied, and craftily avoiding every trap and device that Newell set beside the line to catch him. It was useless to follow his trail, for, except when he is gorged with food and heavy with sleep, one might as well try to run down a caribou as to chase a wide-awake fisher with the hope of catching him.

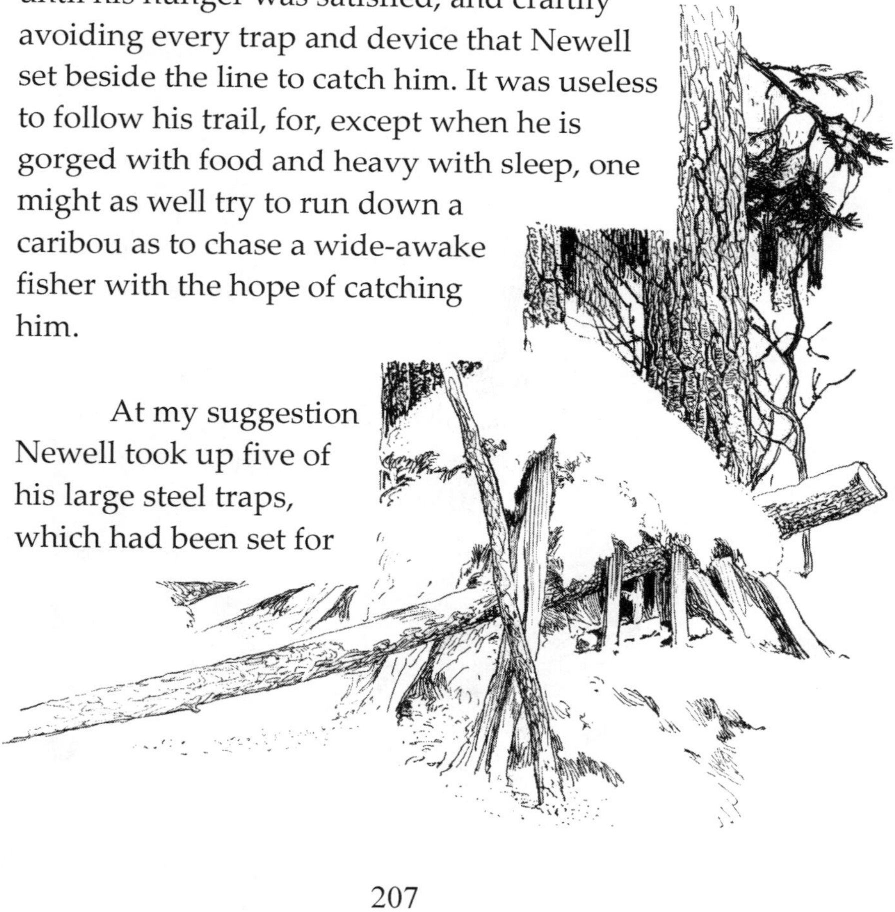

At my suggestion Newell took up five of his large steel traps, which had been set for otter, and we set out one day to outwit Pequam by making him think he understood our devices. At a place in the line where the big fisher's visits had been most frequent we took away the triggers from three of the deadfalls in succession and propped the logs up securely so that they could not fall. The pens were doubled in strength, so that even Pequam could not destroy them; and at the entrance of each pen we placed a steel trap covered over with snow. The two outside traps were left sprung and harmless, but the middle one had its jaws open ready for business; and a' fresh *drag* was made, connecting the three traps and extending out a half mile on either side. My idea was that Pequam would first find one of the outside traps and poke it about cautiously till he was sure it was harmless, and then go straight to the next one.

Farther down the line we tried another device. In the center of a hollow stump we stuck a pole with a fresh-killed rabbit swinging at the top. A row of stakes was then driven about the stump, their tops sharpened and pointing outward, so that Pequam could not reach the stump except through one entrance in the encircling fence. At the entrance we left a steel trap sprung, and covered it carefully with snow; but in the hollow at the top of the stump was another with its hidden jaws wide open, ready for Pequam when he should come to pull down the pole and carry off his prize. During the night a light snow fell and covered up every trace of our work.

Two days later there was an interesting story to read in the snow. Pequam had followed the line till he came to the first steel trap, and instantly he set about understanding the new arrangement. A dozen times he went about the pen, trying every crevice with his nose and eyes. Then he came to the entrance and very carefully scraped away the snow till the harmless trap was bare. He tried it, cautiously at first, with gentle taps and jabs of his paw; then more and more roughly, poking and jerking it about at the end of its chain; but no warning snap followed and nothing happened to hurt him. Whereupon he walked straight over the trap and ate the generous bait that was waiting for him. From here he loped on to the next trap, which was not harmless, and, thinking he understood such things, walked straight into it. We found him near-by with the clog caught fast at the entrance to a den among the rocks.

Long; after I had left the woods I heard from Newell that he had caught another fisher in the top of the hollow stump. Pequam had poked the unset trap about till he knew it was harmless, and then—just as he went to sleep carelessly after killing the deer—had climbed the stump without any thought, apparently, of another pitfall that might be waiting to receive him.

But better than the trapping, and without any regrets, was to wander wide through the woods alone, far away from the saple line, to follow Pequam's trail and see what he caught and where he slept; and then at night, before the singing birch logs, to compare notes with Newell and learn from him the reason for things that I could not understand.

Unlike most wild creatures, Pequam does not seem to keep her little ones with her through the winter. A mother deer usually keeps her fawns until the following spring, breaking a way for them through the heavy snows, leading them to the best feeding places, guarding them from danger, teaching them from her own example the things which a deer must know; and it is one of the sad things of hunting that, if a doe be killed in the autumn, her fawn will have small chance to live through a severe winter, unless, as is sometimes the case, the fawn joins himself to another doe

and follows her about. Even Upweekis the lynx often keeps her big, round-eyed, savage young cubs with her, teaching them to hunt and beat the bush together in the long winter when food is scarce. But Pequam, like all the tribe of weasels, which have scant affection for their young, seems to turn her cubs adrift when she has led them about for a little while in the autumn; after which their instincts and quick wits enable them to shift for themselves.

In the hungry days, however, the fisher cubs let native cunning take the place of affection. The mother may cast them off, but they know her trail, and follow it at a distance whenever they need food. In the early winter they do very well by themselves, though they know little of the world then and are easily caught in traps; but when the spring comes and small game is scarce, and they are neither skillful nor powerful enough to tackle a deer, then they fall back on the skill and generosity of their elders. Sometimes they find their own mother; more often—for Pequam, like Mooweesuk the coon, has a streak of gentleness in him for his own kind—they take up the trail of the first big fisher they cross, and follow it for days to pick the bones and to eat up anything he may have left of his kill after his own hunger is satisfied.

More interesting than these tagging trails of the young fishers are those of the foxes that follow Pequam. Foxes are always hungry, and in the spring, when they are ravenous and when Pequam takes to killing deer on the crust, two or three of them will hang to the trail of a big fisher and live for weeks on the proceeds of his hunting. Pequam rarely covers or hides his kill; but if it be a small one, and the territory be not disturbed by men, he will often lie close beside his game, in the nearest log, and will rush out from his hiding to drive away the prowlers that would not leave a single bone by morning.

Occasionally in the snow you may read the story of his watch and guard, and then a curious thing sometimes comes out. Scarcely has he eaten his full and yawned sleepily when some prowler comes up on his trail to share the feast. If it be another fisher, Pequam stands aside when he is satisfied and makes no objection; for the hungry beggar is a young animal, not yet big enough to kill for himself. The older animals are solitary, each hunting over a wide territory and rarely, except in famine, crossing over to the hunting-grounds of any other fisher; but the young have not yet found their own places, and follow freely where they will. Pequam, if one may believe his tracks, recognizes this and gives his crumbs ungrudgingly to his hungry kinsmen.

"Rouses Pequam's temper"

When the foxes appear you read another story. Before Pequam has half finished they come trotting up on his trail, and squat on their tails in a hungry circle around him. They wrinkle their pointed noses and lick their chops at the good smell in the air; open their jaws in a great hungry yawn, showing their red gums and their sharp white teeth. They are not beggars,—oh, no!—these gaunt, light-footed bandits that with the crows and moose-birds follow Pequam, as a horde of hungry mouths always follow a shark at sea. Sharers of the feast are they, guests from the byways and hedges, to whom every smell is an invitation. Never a word is said; but one sits behind the master of the feast and makes his jaws crack suggestingly; the others move around and yawn prodigiously in his face, telling him politely to hurry up and eat quickly, so that the real feast may begin.

The very sight of these hungry, yawning, exasperating fellows rouses Pequam's temper like poking a stick at him. He rushes at the nearest fox to annihilate him; but Eleemos turns and floats away lightly through the woods, as if the breeze were blowing him. Try as desperately as he will with his short legs, Pequam can never get any nearer to the white tip of the floating plume before him; and worst of it all, Eleemos seems to be making no effort, but looks back over his shoulder as he capers along. Pequam turns back at last, only to hurl himself headlong through the snow far faster than he came; for the other foxes are already on his kill, tearing it away and bolting it in big, hungry mouthfuls. He scatters them like chaff and hunts one away into the swamp; whereupon the first fox slips in and gets a mouthful with the others. Then Pequam comes flying back and sits on his deer and spits impotently at his uninvited guests.

He does not chase them again, but eats his fill, while the foxes sit around and yawn hugely. With a mouthful now to stay their stomachs they can wait a little longer. They are never still a minute, but move around and sit on all sides of the table. When he has eaten enough Pequam cannot quite make up his mind what to do. He is sleepy already and lies down on the deer; but the old habit of hiding away is strong upon him, and he wants to find a hollow log. He cannot sleep where he is, and if he goes away, the foxes will fall upon his game ravenously and leave him only dry pickings when he comes back again. He backs away craftily at last, and then, when a bush hides him and the foxes are tearing at the game, he rushes back and scatters them like a whirlwind.

So the little comedy runs on, and each player writes his own part in the snow for your eyes to read. It always ends the same way. Pequam leaves his game grudgingly and curls him up to sleep in his hollow log. But he slumbers uneasily at first, as one does with something on his mind; and before he can sleep contentedly he must get up once or twice to chivy the foxes, which by this time have eaten their full and are carrying away portions to hide in the woods.

It is perhaps the thought of these hungry thieves—if even a fox can be called a thief for helping himself when he is hungry—that leads Pequam to leave behind him a curious sign of his ownership. Once I found where he had killed a porcupine and left the greater portion of it uneaten. Instead of covering or hiding his game he made, at a little distance, a circle of tracks, going around his game five or six times and leaving as many plain boundary lines in the snow. My first thought at the time—and I hold it still—was that Pequam was a young fisher, and had left a warning to any prowlers that might find his game. When I found it, only a pair of moose-birds had disregarded the warning; but I did not know, at the time, of Pequam's sleepy habit after eating, and it may be that he was somewhere near, drowsing away in a hollow log, and had made the cunning circles of tracks to hide his trail and to confuse any one who should attempt to find him.

It is in hunting the porcupine without injury to himself that Pequam's cunning is most manifest. Unk Wunk is one of the unanswered questions of the wilderness; so stupid, and yet so carefully shielded from the harm and hunger that torments all other creatures. He is always fat, while crafty and powerful beasts are starving; and his armor of pointed quills generally shields him perfectly from their attacks. Occasionally the fox or the lynx or the big owl tackles him, when hunger becomes intolerable and they must eat or die; but to touch the huge chestnut bur anywhere is to fill one's mouth with quills; and behind the bur is the lively tail, always ready to drive in the tormenting barbs by the dozen. Pequam alone has learned the secret of safe attack, and kills a porcupine whenever he is hungry and can find no better meat. Trappers take his skin, but rarely find any deeply imbedded quills to tell of these encounters; while the late winter pelts of fox and lynx often show only too plainly how they have been punished in trying to satisfy their hunger.

A curious trail in the deep snow led me, one day, to what may be the secret of Pequam's success. He had crossed the clumsy trail of a porcupine and loped along it rapidly, till with a rush he headed Unk Wunk before the latter could climb a tree and escape the attack. For not even Pequam would dare follow along a branch and expose his face to the blow of Unk Wunk's tail. The tracks showed that the porcupine had thrust his forehead promptly against a tree to save his face, according to his wont, and then stood ready, a bristling cushion of spears, defying anything to touch him.

Pequam circled swiftly behind his game and plunged into the snow and disappeared. Deep under the deadly tail and the feet and body of Unk Wunk he pushed his tunnel; then thrust his nose out of the snow just under the porcupine's throat and gripped him and held fast. A porcupine never struggles when wounded, but holds his thorny guard till he dies. Pequam, lying under the snow with only his muzzle exposed, so that the barbed and swift-striking tail could not touch him, simply held his grip on the throat till the tense muscles relaxed their spasmodic pull and lay still. Then he came out, opened his game carefully along the under side, where there are no quills, and ate his fill and went away untouched, leaving the briery, untoothsome morsels to any hungry prowlers that might follow his trail to share the feast.

Once since then a guide told me of following a black cat's trail and finding where he crept up on a porcupine and tunneled under him and gripped the throat, while his own body was safe from attack under the snow. And I have no doubt the habit is a more or less common one, and may be witnessed again if one will but follow patiently Pequam's cunning trail. Where fishers increase deer grow scarce, for Pequam kills them easily on the crust; and these two facts—the crusted deer and the outwitted porcupine—undoubtedly explain why Pequam is

often fat even in the gaunt month of March, and why he sleeps well-fed and warm for days at a time while larger or faster animals must wander all night long through the hungry woods.

Many other things were seen or read on the trail of the Cunning One, while Newell followed his lonely saple line, and the little hunting camp on the Dungarvon waited with its warm welcome to tired hunters in the twilight. Those were good days; and no hunting ever paid better in happiness than that which followed the trails without a thought of harm, and was content to let the snow tell its own stories. But, like all good times, they did not last very long. Work called me away; and I like to think that the solitary old Indian sometimes missed his queer hunting companion, who used to go out for caribou and leave his rifle at home, and who always came back satisfied at nightfall.

The door of the little hunting camp now hangs open on its hinges, and within are only mice and squirrels. Newell is far away, following other trails. The birch logs that sang to us the woods' songs are now ashes, and the wind has scattered them to the forest again; but Pequam's coat, still glossy and soft and warm, curls itself into a great muff about a little girl's fingers. The winter wind ruffles it, and it starts and gleams and quivers nervously, as if it heard a footfall on its track; and when you put your face down in it to keep your nose warm, as Pequam used to do when he went to sleep, there is a subtle, woodsy fragrance which speaks of fir balsam and birch smoke, and the still, white woods, and of a warm hollow log under the snow at the end of the crooked trail.

OUT OF THE DEEPS

THE sun was setting gloriously behind the bleak western headlands as our little schooner doubled Goose Cape, nodding a solemn good-night with her jib-boom to the row of solemn seals on the ice floe, and then headed up slowly into the great silent bay to her night's anchorage.

Between us and the unknown waters towered the icebergs, some grounded fast in a hundred fathoms, others drifting majestically in the slow currents, with the long ocean swells racing and breaking over the wide green shelves of ice and *boom-booming* their hollow thunder in the deep caverns. Like a row of mighty sentinels they stretched clear across our course, from the black rocks of Maiden's Arm to the towering cliffs of Bouleaux Cove, forbidding all entrance to the lonely lands and waters beyond. Every crevice and great hollow on their shining sides seemed to be poured full of molten color, while the sunset caught their glittering pinnacles and broke into a glory beyond all words.

Hundreds of sea-birds, gulls and penguins and " hagdowns " and unknown fishers of the deep, had settled upon the icebergs and folded the great wings that were weary with the long day's flight. Here they clustered in a dense mass in some great hollow, like a mother's shoulder, talking softly to one another; more often they settled one by one in an endless line upon the topmost shining ridges, where they stood out like delicate ebony carvings against the rugged roof line of the icebergs. In the whole stupendous scene, rock cliffs and ice mountains and boundless sea and burning sky, the eye came back again and again and rested on these tiny dots against the sunset. The ear heard not the crash of falling ice, nor the roar of the smitten sea, nor the hollow boom of breakers in the caverns; it listened for a low chatter, soft as the talk of birds in their sleep, which spoke of life and the gladness of life in the midst of the vast solitude.

Behind us, as we watched the scene and the *Wild Duck* wore away to find a safe opening between the bergs, the dusk came creeping up over the ocean's brim. In front a marvelous light of sunset and ice and colored sea beckoned yet repelled us by its awful glory. All around us was silence, vast, profound, palpable, a silence of bygone ages, which hushed the sea-birds' chatter and which was only deepened and intensified by the faroff surge of breakers on the shoal and the nearer roll of thunder in the ice caves. Then out of the silence a groan, an awful sound in the primeval stillness of the place, rumbled over the startled sea. It was as if the abyss itself, silent for untold ages, had at last found voice, and the voice was a moan of pain.

The man at the wheel, a grizzled old fisherman of St. Barbes, who took sublimity and cod traps, storm and sunshine, roaring sea and the sweet rest of snug harbors all alike in seasoned indifference, whirled sharply and swept the sea with a glance like a needle thrust. Joe the cook tumbled up from the forecastle, his mouth open to take everything in.

" What 's that, boy ? " he demanded of the skipper with the freedom of Newfoundland fishermen; but the skipper only shook his head, and looked seaward whence the sound had come.

" Breakers on Brehaut Shoal," said the man at the wheel doubtfully at last. " Air in the ice caves," echoed Jack; but at

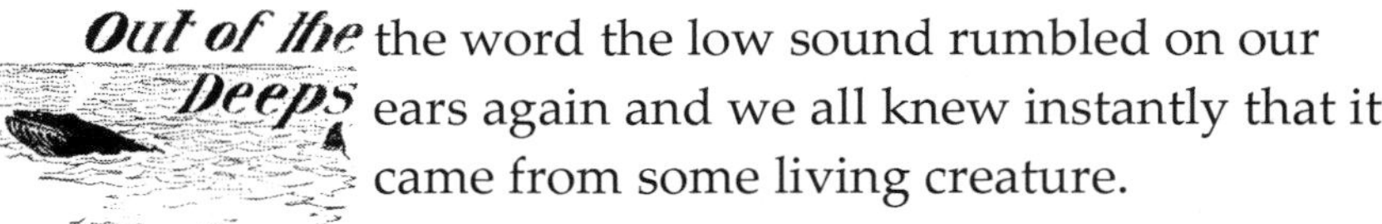

the word the low sound rumbled on our ears again and we all knew instantly that it came from some living creature.

Noel the Indian pointed suddenly to windward, where a hump of water separated itself from the sea and swirled and bubbled like soup in a pot. A huge whale broke the surface; something flashed beside it; then another surge and the whale was gone; but the awful moan was in our ears again. On the instant all discipline was lost in a great curiosity as I grabbed the wheel from the grizzled old fisherman, while he and Noel tugged at the mainsheet, and the skipper jumped for the jibs, and the cook ran for the skipper's glass, and the little *Wild Duck* whirled up to the wind and went poking her jib-boom at the soapy lather where the whale had disappeared.

Now a whale is so big that puny men may be pardoned the supposition that he has no ordinary feelings. All the way up the West Coast and through the Straits, where we had struggled against tide and gale and fog and ice and the deadly monotony of cramped limbs and close quarters, my friend had amused himself by shooting bullets at the whales that crossed our course, as one would chuck peas at an elephant. Since we could rarely get near enough to study the huge creatures it was fun to stir them up, and watch the sea " seethe like a pot " when they went down in a hurry. A repeating rifle was usually standing by the foremast, with which we sometimes added a dish to our fare of cod and lobsters, and which served Noel well in bagging a young seal for its oil and skin. As the schooner lay balanced for hours at a time between wind and tide, and we saw with weariness another day without gain and another salmon river unexplored, there would be a sudden *whoosh,* like the breath of forty locomotives, and a great black back would come plunging up out of the depths. Then the weariness would vanish, and all watched intently as somebody grabbed the rifle and sent the bullets skipping. Invariably they did no harm at all, but only waked us up; for the huge black back would go ponderously on its way, rising and sinking, with bullets skipping like hornets athwart its path and lighting everywhere except on the shining hump. When the magazine was exhausted Noel would chuckle silently and go to sleep again.

The whales were about us continually in all shapes and sizes, only a few of which were familiar; the rest plunged into soundless deeps or followed their own endless trails into the fog, like strange steamers, unknown and unnamed. Now a shoal of playing dolphins would go rushing, rolling past with a purring roar of smitten water like the low surge of breakers on the beach; while over the mad stampede single individuals hurled themselves into the air in sheer exuberance of life and animal spirits. Again a troop of little whales of some unknown species would gather silently around the fishing punts, spying and peeking, as inquisitive as so many blue jays. Once a stray right-whale, and again an unmeasured monster—a sulphur-bottom, I judged, from his enormous length and his high spouting—steamed past like an express train, making the *Wild Duck* seem of no size or consequence whatever. Sometimes a dozen of the leviathans would be in sight at once; again a solitary rorqual would cross our bows ponderously, always alone, yet maintaining apparently a secret communication with others of his kind scattered over twenty miles of ocean; for, though I never saw them approach each other, they always appeared and vanished, turning to east or west all together, as if a single impulse were leading them. Knowing little about the uncouth creatures, I contented myself with classifying them all, as sailors do, into big ones and little ones, and would watch for hours in the hope of getting near enough to one to observe him closely. Meanwhile my friend and the sailors were rapidly and harmlessly going through the supply of cartridges.

One day, when from an enormous depth a big whale shot his length up out of the sea and fell back with a resounding splash and shot the air out of his lungs with a *whoosh* to waken the seven sleepers, I grabbed the rifle thoughtlessly—having jibed at the others for their poor shooting—and took a quick crack at the monster before he had fairly settled down to travel. The steel-jacketed bullet caught him fair on the hump, glanced through, and went skipping out exultingly over the sea. Then, so quick that it made one rub his eyes, the huge form had disappeared and the sea thereabouts looked like a basin of soap-suds. "B 'ys, b'ys, but that tickled his backbone!" cried the skipper; but for me, at least, one problem was solved effectually. The whale has feelings, no doubt about that; and for the rest of the trip the rifle was kept in the cabin and we began to watch the huge creatures with a less barbaric interest.

Another day, towards twilight, while the schooner loafed along in no hurry whatever to reach an anchorage, I was standing at the bow watching the shoals of fish and the circling gulls, when

Out of the Deeps

a whale broke water and lay resting on the sea. Close about him were some black rocks, breaking the surface as the tide fell; and as Leviathan scratched himself leisurely, like a huge sea-pig, against the rough surfaces to rid his skin of the clinging barnacles, or lay quiet with his black hump above the water-line, he might easily have been mistaken for one of the rocks, about which the tide was swirling and ebbing. A big herring gull, heavy and sleepy with too much feeding, came flapping along. As he saw the inviting rock he set his broad wings and dropped his heavy feet to alight. The toes had barely touched the huge back when—*plunge ! kuk-kuk !* There was a lightning swirl and a smother of soapy water. The whale was gone; and a frightened and wide-awake gull was jumping upward, humping his back and threshing the air and *kukkuking* his astonishment at the disappearance of his late landing-place.

Here were more feelings, delicate enough to feel the touch of a bird's toes on a back so big that, judging by what the whalemen had told me of the whale's insensibility while being lanced, I had supposed its nerves must be arranged about as plentifully as telegraph wires in the country. The whole proceeding was like the lightning jump of a sleeping wolf when a twig cracks, or a leaf drops close to his ear.

One day, while the schooner lay becalmed, I jumped into the dory with Noel and pulled inshore to see what the herring boats were doing, and to collect some of the queer, unknown fish that were brought up in the nets. As we moved among the boats I caught sight of a big whale gliding in towards us with all the cautiousness of a coyote approaching a sleeping camp. He would stop here and there and pick up something, and glide forward again to left or right, like a fox quartering towards a quail roost. As he drew near I saw that he was after the scattered herring which had fallen from the nets, and which were now floating astern on the surface as the tide drifted them away. Closer and closer he came, while we all stopped our work to watch. The huge bulk would glide softly up to a tiny dot of silver floating on the ocean's blue; the great mouth would open, wide enough to take in a fisherman, and close gently over one small herring. Then he would swallow his tidbit and back away slowly to watch the boats awhile before picking up another morsel. He always turned sidewise so as to look at us with one eye, as a chicken does; for he seemed unable to see straight in front of him. But he had other senses to depend upon, and also that unknown feeling of danger when ordinary senses are useless, which the whalemen tell us is so strongly developed in this uncouth monster. While he was nosing after two or three herring I motioned Noel to be quiet, and slipping an oar over the stern began to scull gently towards, him. Hardly had the bow of my dory cleared the line of punts when he sank from sight; and when he came up again he was far away and heading straight out to sea.

Farther up the coast, where the Straits began to be ice choked, another curious fact carrie out, namely, that some of these warmblooded monsters, though they live amid the icebergs, are unwilling to come close to even a small cake of floating ice. The water there is always chilled, and Leviathan avoids it absolutely. More than that, though he is generally set down as a stupid creature, he showed some small degree of intelligence in taking care of himself. Here on the West Coast, especially under the influence of strong southerly winds, the tide will often set for days in the same direction without turning. Leviathan knows this, though many a skipper loses his vessel in the fog because of his ignorance of this steady eastward set of the tide. At such times the loose ice drifts away and the whales enter many of the narrow bays to feed abundantly on the shoaling fish. But when the tide turns at last, and the ice comes drifting back, the huge creatures leave the bays, fearing to be shut in by a barrier of ice to the whalemen's mercies. And though there be a dozen whales in the bay, as many miles apart, they generally turn all at the same instant, as if at command, and head swiftly out to the open sea and safety.

Where the Straits grew narrow and the floating ice threatened to block our way altogether, we saw another curious bit of Leviathan's precaution. He would stand straight up on end, appearing like a huge black spile rising ten or fifteen feet above the water, and look far ahead over the nearer ice floes to see if the Straits were blocked. And if the survey were unsatisfactory, he would dive deep and come up with a terrific rush, breaching his entire length out of water, for one swift look far ahead to see whether his course were clear.

Still later, when we had at last doubled Cape Bauld with its fog and ice and were heading southward, I saw, one day, a mother whale lying on the sea suckling her little one. They were resting inshore, close beside our course, and I had an excellent chance to watch them through my glasses ere the mother took alarm and disappeared silently, as a mother moose might have done, leading her ungainly offspring. To my wonder she did not lie sleepily quiet, as other mothers do,"—that would have been fatal to the little fellow,—but kept up a rhythmic rolling from side to side; now dipping the calf deep from sight, now lifting his head above the top of the waves as he clung to her side, so as to give him free chance to breathe as he fed greedily from his mother's great breast. And as we drew nearer there was a faint, low mumbling,—whether the rare voice of the whale, or an audible breathing through the blow-holes, or made in some other way, I could not tell,—full of a deep, uncouth tenderness as she talked in her own way to her little one, telling the world also that even here, in the cold, ice-choked wastes of desolation, life was good, for love was not lacking. Indeed, the tenderness and rare devotion of these huge monsters for their little ones is the most fascinating thing about them.

Here were feelings of an entirely different sort; and now the heart of man was touched in the thought that there was something in the huge creatures of our sport that was, after all, akin to ourselves. At first our interest had been largely barbaric, to stir up Leviathan with the fear of man, and to see how quickly, like the oily flash of a dolphin, he could make his bulk disappear. The scientific stage followed, in which we spoke of unclassified varieties, hoping to make a

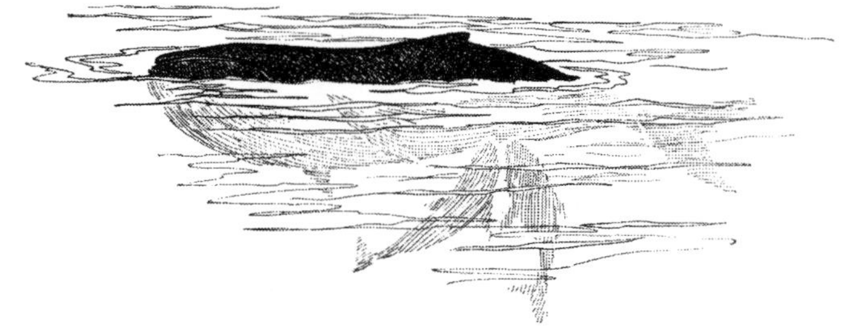

discovery, and babbled of *Denticete* (the presence of teeth being more important than habits of life) and *Balaenidae* and *Physeteridae,* especially *Physeter macrocephalus,* and *Orcinus gladiator* in six varieties—

" Wat 's that ? " demanded the grizzled old fisherman, who could stand it no longer.

" That 's a killer-whale," I told him.

"Oh," said he, "sh'ld think 't would kill ye to remember it."

So we gave up trying to name these monsters of the abyss with names sufficiently uncouth to be scientific, and brought back the crew to life by lowering a boat to see what kind of squid or fish or tiny mollusk they were eating. For we had been told that, in certain species, the throat of one of these huge whales is so small that a pippin would choke him.

Soon the sporting interest awoke. One who knew the whalemen well talked of harpoons and ambergris, and told the story of the Nantucket ship that had been charged, and battered and sunk, by a fighting old bull. Whereupon the grizzled fisherman of St. Barbes put in with an account of what he had seen last summer, when a whale blundered into the fishermen's nets during a storm. Three days he lay in the trap; now pushing his head into a net and

"A long snaky body leaped clear of the water"

drawing back in afright at the queer thing; now breaching clear of the water to see if there were any way out, and falling back heavily again as if discouraged in his quest. Then he evidently made up what he would call his mind, and the whole fleet of boats stood by and cursed impotently while the hopes of a dozen families went whirling blindly out to sea on the flukes of a bewildered rorqual. But all these stages were passed; and our interest was purely human as we stood now in a close group at the weather rail of the schooner, scholar and fisherman alike, to learn what hidden grief or pain had added a new voice to the world of waters.

The whale rolled up again, nearer this time. There was a wriggle and flash beside him; a long snaky body leaped clear of the water, doubling itself like a steel spring, and struck down a terrific blow at the whale's head. "Thresher!" cried the skipper excitedly. The creature leaped and struck again, and a heavy thud rolled over the ocean, like the blow of a giant flail. Before I could see plainly all that happened something struck the whale from below, and he rolled under in a smother of foam, while the ocean itself seemed to bellow forth its rage and pain. But whether the strange sound were indeed the rare voice of the whale, or the reverberation of smitten water, or the vibration of great volumes of air driven out of the laboring lungs through the blow-holes, we could not tell; nor had the fishermen ever heard it save when a whale was fighting for his life.

While the whale was gone and we watched breathless for him to come to the surface again, the skipper and the old fisherman answered my hurried questions. Yes, they had seen the threshers, or fox-sharks, before, and had sometimes caught them in their nets. Once they had seen three or four of them fighting a whale as they were jigging cod on the shoals. They were from twelve to twenty feet long, the skipper said, including the prolonged upper lobe of the tail, which they could use with terrific force as a weapon of offense. Then the scholar brought out of the cabin the skull of a fox-shark that we had found in the hut of a Labrador fisherman, a skull that was chiefly a pair of long, pointed, cruel jaws with rows of hooked ivory fangs fitting together like the teeth of a bear trap. "That's it,—a thresher," said the skipper. "He'll gouge them jaws into a whale or porp'se with a twist o' his tail, and rip out a bite that would fill a bucket. There he is ! "

The whale shot out of the depths and breached clear of the water in his upward rush. As he fell back there was the same flash and wriggle beside him, the same leap as of a bent spring, the same heavy blow and moan. Then something else appeared, darting up like a ray of light, and the long blade of a swordfish ripped through the whale's side. The

force of his attack brought the big fish to the surface, where we saw his shoulders plainly and caught the flash of light on his terrible weapon as he turned to dive beneath his victim. The whale sounded again, turning fair on end, with the thresher leaping over him, or standing on his head to strike down a last terrible blow, as the huge victim sought blindly for an abyss deep enough to escape the lash and sting of his enemies.

The schooner fell away in the light evening wind, and the rush of the uncouth tragedy carried it swiftly away where no man watched the end of it. But this much seemed clear: the two strangely assorted bandits, savage monsters of the savage sea, were working together to destroy their great and helpless victim,—the thresher lashing him down to the swordfish with flail-like blows of his flukes, and the swordfish driving him up on the point of his lance to the thresher again. What started the fight, or how it ended, no man can say. Here and there, between the ship and the rim of dusk, there would be a sudden turmoil, a flash and a whirl of foam. As the turmoil sank, a low moan shivered on the sea. So they passed out into the deeps and were gone.

MATWOCK
OF THE ICEBERGS

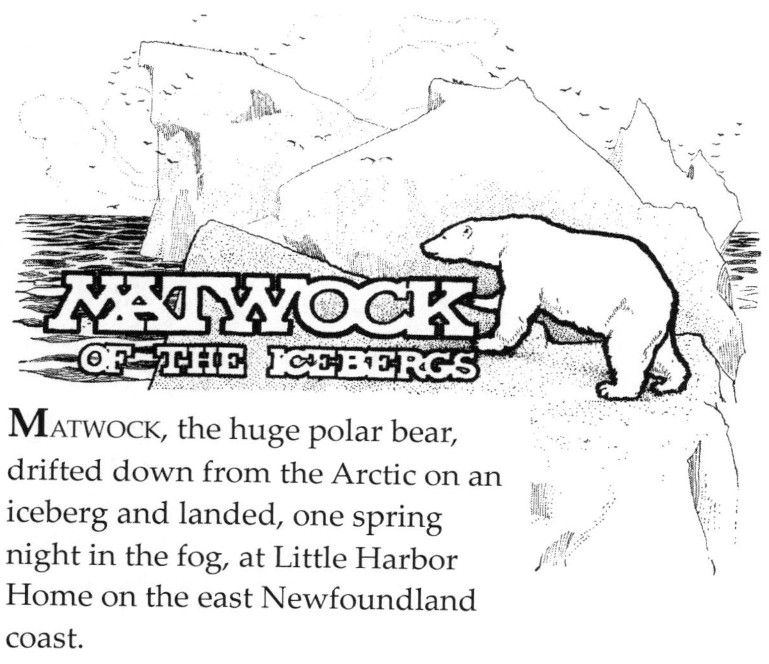

MATWOCK, the huge polar bear, drifted down from the Arctic on an iceberg and landed, one spring night in the fog, at Little Harbor Home on the east Newfoundland coast.

It seemed at first a colossal fatality, that iceberg. The fishermen had just brought their families back from the winter lodge in the woods, and had made their boats ready to go out to the Hook-and-Line Grounds for a few fresh cod to keep themselves alive. Then a heavy fog shut in, and in the midst of the fog the iceberg came blundering into the tickle, as if there were no other place in a thousand leagues of sea and rock-bound coast. There were two hundred fathoms of water at the harbor mouth, and the great berg touched bottom softly, yet with a terrific impact which sent huge masses of ice crashing down on the black rocks on either side. It might stay a month, or it might drift away on the next tide. Meanwhile the fishermen were helpless as flies in a bottle; for the iceberg corked the harbor mouth and not even a punt could get out or in.

Old Tomah came that same day from his hunting camp far away in the interior. Grown tired of eating beaver meat and smoking willow bark, he had brought some otter skins to trade for a little pork and tobacco, with a few warm stockings thrown in for good measure. But the trading schooner, for which the islanders watch in spring as a lost man watches for morning, had not yet come, and the fishermen were themselves at the point of starvation. For a month they had tasted nothing but a little dried fish and doughballs. Hunting was out of the question; for their dogs were all dead, and their few guns were out with the young men, who before the advent of the iceberg had taken their lives in their hands and gone up the coast sealing in a stout little schooner. So Tomah, taking his otter skins, started back for his own camp.

As his custom was in a strange place, Tomah first climbed the highest hill in the neighborhood to get his bearings. The blundering iceberg seemed to him a grim joke, more grim than the joke on himself which had left him after a forty-mile tramp without pork or tobacco or warm stockings. He was watching the berg with silent, Indian intentness when a mass of overhanging ice crashed down on the rocks. Something stirred in a deep cave suddenly laid open; the next instant his keen eyes made out the figure of a huge white bear standing in the cave, rocking his head up and down as the smell of the village drifted out of the harbor into his hungry nostrils.

Tomah came down from the hill to leave a warning at the little store. " Bes' look out," he said. "Bear over dere on dat hice, big, oh, big one! He come here to-night, soon's dark, see wat he kin find. He hungry, an' oh, cross; don't 'fraid noting. Bes' set urn trap, ketch urn plenty meat." Then, because he had left his own gun behind and could borrow none in the village, he started inland on his long tramp.

Matwock the bear landed from his iceberg as soon as it was dark, as Tomah had said, and headed straight for the village. For a month he had been adrift in the open sea without food; because the seals, which had first enticed him away till fifty miles of open water stretched between him and his native haunts, had now

returned to the coast to rear their young on the rocks and grounded ice-floes. Meanwhile the great berg to which he clung, as a mariner to a floating spar, drifted steadily southward over the mist-shrouded ocean with its base a thousand feet deep in a powerful current. Most of the time he had slept, going back to the old bear habit of hibernation to save his strength; but when the berg grounded, and the wind from the harbor brought the smell of fish and of living animals to his nostrils, he sprang up ravenously hungry. Never having seen men, he had no fear. Straight and swift he followed his nose, ready to seize the first food, living or dead, that lay in his path.

On the outskirts of the village he came upon a huge deadfall which the men had made hurriedly at Tomah's suggestion, partly to get meat, of which they were in sore need, but more to protect themselves and their little ones from the savage prowler which knew no fear. The bait was a lot of offal,—bones, and fish-skins tied together with cod-line; and the fall log was the stump of a big mast, water-logged and heavy as lead, which had come ashore years ago from a wreck, and which they made heavier still by rocks lashed on with cables. Matwock entered the pen swiftly, grabbed the bait, and *thud!* down came the weighted log on his shoulders.

Now a black bear would have been caught across the small of the back and his spine cracked like an egg-shell by the fearful blow. But Matwock was altogether too big, and the pen altogether too small. With a roar of rage he hurled the log aside, smashed the pen into fragments, and charged straight through the village, knocking to pieces with blows of his terrible paws the pens and fish-flakes that stood across his path. More than one man jumped from his bed at the uproar to see the huge white brute rush past, and to bless himself that he was safe within doors.

Matwock went back to his cave in the iceberg, angry and sore, yet with a strange timidity at heart from this first experience in the abodes of men. What the abominable thing was that had fallen on his back he had, of course, no idea; but he had learned in a minute that he could not prowl here with the power and authority that marked him in the vast snowy solitudes where no man dwells. He was licking a wound that a chain had torn in his shaggy white coat, when a faint scratching and grunting, amid ceaseless roar of breakers and booming of waves in the ice caverns, came to his sensitive ears and made him steal out instantly to investigate.

Down on a shelf of ice, on the seaward side of the great berg, two bull seals had

floundered out, fat and heavy with food, to sleep and bask in the sun, which was just then rising. A glance told the bear that the big seals had chosen the spot well, where no danger could approach save from the open sea out of which they had just come. Of the berg itself they had no fear whatever; for it rose behind them a hundred feet in a sharp incline to where a score of glistening spires and minarets began, on which the sea-birds were resting. So they stretched their fat bulks comfortably on the narrow shelf of ice, watching the open sea, blinking sleepily in the sunshine.

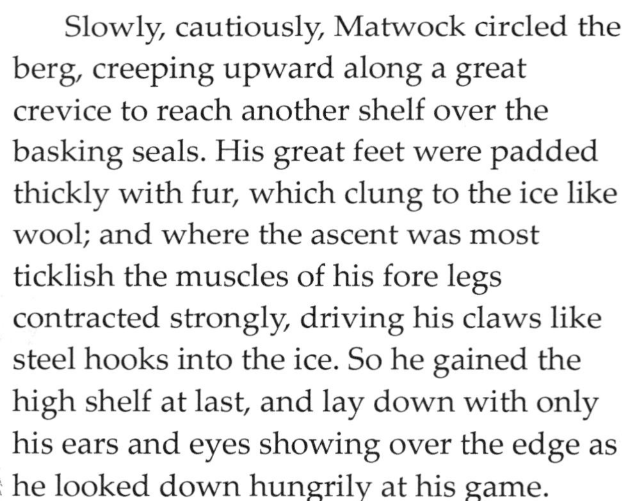

Slowly, cautiously, Matwock circled the berg, creeping upward along a great crevice to reach another shelf over the basking seals. His great feet were padded thickly with fur, which clung to the ice like wool; and where the ascent was most ticklish the muscles of his fore legs contracted strongly, driving his claws like steel hooks into the ice. So he gained the high shelf at last, and lay down with only his ears and eyes showing over the edge as he looked down hungrily at his game.

Below him was a dizzy incline, steep as a mountain top, polished and glistening with the frost and storms of the centuries, at the foot of which the unconscious seals were basking. Very deliberately Matwock chose his position over the larger seal; then with his hind legs he pushed himself steadily over the edge, crouching low on his belly with his nose on his fore paws, which were stretched straight out in front of him. Like a flash of light he glanced down over the slope, striking the seal a terrific blow and knocking him end over end as the bear shot over him into the sea. There was a terrible commotion for an instant, which set the sea-birds flap ping and clamoring wildly; then out of the turmoil Matwock's head arose, gripping the big seal by the neck. He laid his game carefully on the ice shelf, kicked himself up after it, and ate it there, where a moment before it had been blinking sleepily in the morning sun.

The presence of his favorite game in the strange land turned Matwock's thoughts from the village of men into which he had blundered with the iceberg. No boats came out or in to disturb him, so he kept his abode in the ice cavern, which was safe and warm, and out of which he wandered daily up and down the rocky coast.

A few mother seals had their young here, hidden on the great ice-floes, which were fast anchored to the rocks and shoals. The little seals are snow-white at first—for kind Nature forgets none of her helpless children—the better to hide on the white ice on which they are born. Only their eyes and the tips of their noses are black, and at the first alarm they close their eyes and lie very still, so that it is almost impossible to see them. Even when you stand over them they look like rough lumps of snow-ice. If they have time they even hide the black tips of their noses in their white fur coats; and if you appear suddenly they simply close their eyes, and the black nose tip looks like a stray pebble or a tiny bit of bark left by the uneasy winds that sweep over the ice-floes. As they grow larger and begin to fish for themselves they gradually turn dark and sleek, like their mothers, the better to slip unseen through the dark waters in which they hunt.

Like all bears, Matwock had poor eyes, and depended chiefly on his nose in scouting. He would swim swiftly, mile after mile, along the edges of the floes, raising his head to sniff every breeze, trying to locate where the young seals were hiding. But the little ones give out almost no scent at such times, besides being invisible, and Matwock rarely dined on a nest of young seals. The only way he could catch them was by a cunning bit of bear strategy. He would swim far out from the edge of the floes and drift about among the floating ice, looking himself like an ice cake; or else he would crouch on an ice-field and watch for hours till he saw a big seal clamber out, and

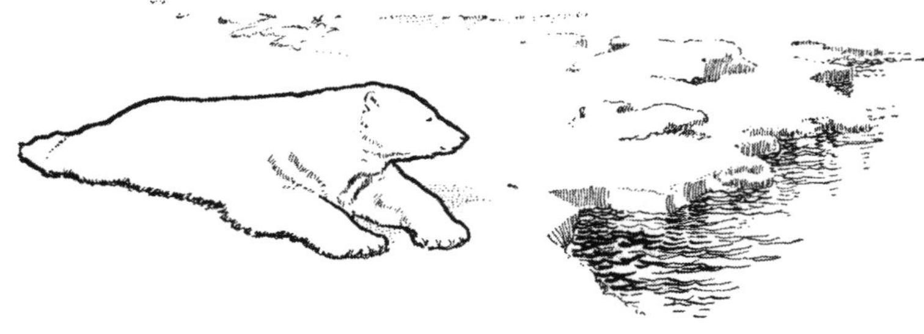

knew from her actions that she was feeding her young. Then he would head straight and swift for the spot and nose all over it till he found what he was seeking.

When the big bull seals came ashore to bask in the sun, resting on a rock or the edge of an ice-floe whence they could slip instantly into deep water, Matwock invented a new style of still-hunting. He would slip silently far down to leeward—for the seal's nose is almost as keen as his own—and there begin his cautious stalk up-wind. Sinking his enormous weight deep in the water till only his nose and the top of his head appeared, he would glide slowly along the edge of the floe, looking exactly like a bit of loose ice drifting along in the tide. When near the game he would disappear entirely and, like an otter, not a ripple marked the spot where he went down.

The big seal would be blinking sleepily on the edge of the ice-floe, raising himself on his flippers to stretch like a wolf, or turning leisurely to warm both sides at the sun, when the huge head and shoulders of a bear would shoot up out of the water directly in front of him. One swift, crushing blow of the terrible paw, and the seal would be dead without a thought of what had happened to him.

So Matwock lived and hunted for a week, growing fat and contented again. Then the seals vanished on one of their sudden migrations—following the fish, no doubt—and for a week more he hunted without a mouthful. One night, when he returned late to his cave, the great iceberg had broken its anchorage and drifted well out of the tickle, and from the harbor the smell of fresh fish drifted into his hungry nostrils. For the day had been sunny and calm, and the starving fishermen had slipped out to the Hook-and-Line Grounds and brought back exultingly the first cod of the season.

Again Matwock came ashore, tired as he was after an all-day's swim, and headed straight for the good smell in the village. The big deadfall was set in his path, baited with fresh offal, and the log was weighted twice as heavily as before. But the bear had learned cunning and entered the trap from the rear, tearing the heavy pen to pieces as if it were made of straws. The fall came down again with a thud that made the ground shiver; but it fell harmlessly on the bed log, and Matwock ate the bait greedily to the last scrap. Then he entered the village, rummaging the wharves and sheds boldly, and leaving his great footprints at every door. When he had eaten everything in sight he headed down the Long Arm of the harbor, drawn still by the smell of fish that floated up in the still night air.

Late that night Old Tomah appeared with his otter skins and a haunch of caribou at Daddy Crummet's cabin, on the edge of the woods far down at the bottom of Long Arm. All winter Daddy Crummet had been sick, chiefly from rheumatism and lack of food; and Tomah, taking pity on the lonely old man, blundered around in the dark to find wood to make a stew of the savory meat which he had brought with him all the way from his camp in the interior. At twilight a fisherman—kind-hearted and generous, as they all are—had come to leave a couple of fresh cod and hurry away again on his long, weary pull up the Arm. Daddy meant to cook the fish, but was too weak when the time came, and left them in a barrel in his little shed. Then came Tomah with his stew, and the old man ate and felt better. It was midnight when they had smoked a pipe of Tomah's dried willow bark and traded the scant news from the two ends of the wilderness and turned in to sleep.

A terrible racket in the shed roused them—*whack ! bang ! thump !* Something was out there knocking everything to pieces. Daddy, under the bedclothes, began to shiver and wail that the devil himself had come to fetch him. Tomah tumbled out of his caribou skins and jumped up like a jack-in-a-box, just as a barrel was flung against the door with a crash that made it shiver. In the appalling silence that followed they heard the *p'chap, p'chap* of some huge beast crunching the codfish between his jaws.

Tomah had brought his gun this time. He grabbed it from behind the stove, pulled the big hammer back, and felt with his fingers to be sure that the cap was ready on the nipple. He stole to the door and opened it cautiously, pushing the gun-barrel out ahead of him. A huge white beast turned swiftly as the door squeaked. Tomah, making out what seemed to him a great head in the darkness, poked the muzzle of the gun into it and pulled the trigger. There was a deafening roar; the door was slammed back in the face of the old Indian with a force that sent him sprawling on his back. Daddy with a last terrible groan lay still, as if it were all over.

When Tomah scrambled to his feet, his ears ringing, his nose filled with pungent powder smoke, there lay Matwock at the end of his long trail. He was lying as if asleep, his great paws outspread across the threshold, his head resting heavily between them. The tail of the last codfish stuck out of a corner of his mouth, and his lips were parted in a ferocious grin, as if to the end it were all a huge joke.

" Py cosh !" said Tom ah, rubbing his scalp and looking down in a puzzled way at the great beast "why I go lug um dat caribou forty mile, huh ? Plenty meat here—oh, plenty!" he added, as he dragged the great head aside, and shut the door, and rolled up in his caribou skins for another nap.

WHERE THE
SALMON JUMP

Where the Salmon Jump

A GLORIOUS salmon river, unnamed but not unknown to the few Newfoundland fishermen who have explored the rugged East Coast, comes singing and shouting down through the woods and leaps hilariously over Kopswaugan, the jumping place. Below the falls the river roars and tumbles among the great rocks; spreads a little into numerous channels of rushing white water; gathers again into a strong, even, rippling current, full of crinkly yellow lights; rolls through a huge pool sedately; and then goes shouting down the rapids to another fall. Birds are singing to the swelling buds; the wind rustles among the new leaves and hums steadily in the spruce tops; the air quivers to the rhythmic throbbing of the falls; a deep organ peal rolls up from the rapids; but all these sounds and subtle harmonies are but dreams of the sleeping woods,—for listen! over all broods the unbroken silence of the wilderness.

Just below the falls, where the torrent spreads into hurrying white channels, a man with a salmon rod is standing on a flat rock that juts into the current. All the bright sunny morning he has been standing there, his ears full of bird and river music, his eyes full of the rushing foam and sunlight of the river, his heart brimful of all that is good in the wilderness. A couple of salmon, little nine-pounders, lie on a shaded mossy bank, where Noel sits smoking his pipe. Now and then the Indian quietly advises trying a pool lower down; and the advice is good, because the river is full of salmon, and down below, where they have not seen the fly, they will come up with a rush at anything. Here they have already grown shy from seeing the little Jock Scott sweeping over the foam, followed by the terrific rushes of two captured salmon and of three more that broke away gloriously. But it is only a small part of fishing to catch fish, and the man finds it perfect where he is, thinking it better fun to locate one good salmon and entice him to rise, rather than go below and catch or lose a dozen. So he stands quietly on the jutting rock, watching the river, listening to the music.

So long has he stood there, following the swing and jump of his little fly in the boiling current, that the rushing movement has got into his eyes, producing a curious illusion that every salmon fisher will recognize. Not only the river, but the shores themselves seem sweeping along to keep pace with the hurrying flood. The big log that bridges the stream below the falls is running swiftly away, and after it come the white sheet and thunder of the waterfall trying to catch it. The green banks and bushes scud away like clouds before the wind. Even the great solid rock under foot joins the swift, unsteady procession; and down we all go, trees, rocks, and river, swaying, jumping, singing, and shouting together on a glorious chase through the wilderness.

In the midst of the rush and tumult the clear, sweet song of Killooleet, the white-throated sparrow, follows us, as if he were saying, *Good-by, Friend Fisherman, Fisherman, Fisherman*. And, spite of all the apparent uproar of rocks and river, the exquisite little melody sounds in our ears as clearly as if Killooleet were singing behind our tent in the twilight stillness.

The man's head grows dizzy with the delusion. His foothold, at best, is none too steady over the rushing torrent; so he closes his eyes to bring back the reality of things. And the reality must be good indeed, judging by the way his soul, like a wind-touched harp, is thrilling to the melody of woods and waters.

As he opens his eyes again there is a sudden plunge on the edge of the farthest white rush of water. A huge salmon tumbles into sight, showing head and shoulders and a foot of broad blue back that makes the man's nine-pounders look like smelts in a cod trap.

"Das de feller; big, oh, big one!" says Noel, straightening his back, and instantly the slender rod gets into action. The fly falls softly across the current; swings clown with the flood and fetches up beautifully at the end of a straight leader, just over the spot where the water humped itself as the big salmon went down. Like a flash he boils up at the lure, throwing his big shoulders out of the foam in his rush; but the fly swings nearer and hangs skittering on the surface.

" Miss um, dat time," says Noel with immense disappointment; and the man draws in his line and sits clown on the rock to let the big salmon settle into his sunken eddy and forget what he saw when his head came out of water.

While we are waiting for him to grow—resting him," the salmon fishermen call it—let us find out, if we can, what he is doing here, and why he halts so long in the midst of all this turmoil, while his instincts are calling him steadily up the river to the quiet shallows where his life began.

First, look down into the water there at your feet, where the river is running swiftly but smoothly over the yellow pebbles near shore. Nothing but smiles, dimples, and crinkly yellow lights, whirling and changing ceaselessly, as if the river here were full of liquid sunshine. Look again; curve a hand on either side of your eyes to shut out the side-lights, and look steadily just below that round yellow stone under its three feet of crinkly sunshine. At first you see nothing, your eyes being full of the flashing surfaces and the dimpling lights and shadows of the yellow flood. Suddenly, as if a window were opened in the river, you see a vague quivering outline. " Did he just come? Is he gone again?" ' Not at all; he is right there; look again.

Another long look; again the impression of a window opened, and now you see a salmon plainly. He is lying there, with his nose in a sunken eddy, resting quietly while the river rolls on over him. You see his shining silver sides, the blue tint on his back, the black line of a net on his head, the tail swaying rhythmically,—every line of the splendid fish as in a clear photograph. Then, as if the window were suddenly shut, you see nothing but dancing yellow lights. The fish has vanished utterly, and you must look again and again, waiting till the lights and dimples run away together; and there is your salmon, lying just where he was before; nor has he moved, except for the lazy swaying of his broad tail and the balancing of his fins, while the lights above hid him from your eyes.

When looking for salmon, as with other good things in life, the eye is easily confused by a multitude of little, unimportant things close at hand. Standing on the same rock Noel will point out a score of salmon where you see nothing but changing lights and dimples. It is not because his eyes are stronger or keener than yours—for they would fail in a week if they had your work to do—but simply because he has learned to look through the intermediate superficialities for the better thing that he is seeking. Where your eye sees only ripples and flashes, his eye disregards these things and finds the big salmon lying just below them.

Climb into the tree there, the big spruce leaning out over the water. Now the surface lights have lost their power over your eyes, and you can see clearly to the river's bed. There, close beside the one salmon that you glimpsed for a moment, a dozen more are lying. Above and below they sprinkle the river, each one lying with his nose behind a stone and catching the current's force

on his fins in such a way that the flood, which would sweep him away, is made to hold him in position without conscious effort, just as a sea-gull soars against the wind.

Look out now at the white rush where the big salmon just plunged at my fly. He is not there, and you wonder if the shining leader or the sight of the swaying rod has scared him away. Now let your eye follow the current a little way. There, ten feet below where the foam ceases, a monster salmon is lying behind a stone under a smooth run of water. As you look he darts forward like a ray of light; you lose him for an instant; then he plunges out just where you saw his first great rise. In a moment he sweeps back again and rounds up into his own eddy, lightly, gracefully, as a sloop rounds up to her mooring. There is something in his mouth,—a leaf perhaps, or a big black and yellow butter fly,—but the next moment he shoots it out, as one would blow a cloud of smoke. The current seizes, crumples it, and sends it down, spreading and quivering like a living thing, into the next eddy. Instantly another salmon flashes into sight, catches the leaf with a whirl and plunge, holds it in his mouth a moment and then blows it out again.

That 's what they are doing, just playing with pretty little things that come skipping and dancing down the river, as your fly came at the end of its invisible leader. Half an hour ago they were asleep, or utterly indifferent to all your flies and delicate casting; now the queer mood is on them again, and they will take anything you offer. But wait a moment; here comes a fish-hawk.

Ismaques, on set wings, comes sailing gently down the river. He sheers off with a sharp *ch'wee!* and circles twice as he notices us in the tree-top; but in a moment he is scanning the water again. From his height his keen eyes see every fish in the river; but they are all too large and too deep under the swift water. Later, when the run of grilse comes in, he will be able to pick up a careless one; but now he just looks over the river, as if it were his own preserve, and circles back to the lake where his nest is. When he brings his little ones down here to fish, you will see them at first whirling low over the water, all excitement at seeing so many big salmon for the first time. But the ripples and the dancing lights bother their eyes, just as they do yours; and then you will hear Ismaques whistling them up higher where they can see better.

As we stand on the rock once more and the fly goes sweeping down the current, there is the same swift rush of our big salmon in the same spot, and another miss. He is rising short, that is, behind the fly; which shows that he is a bit suspicious, and that our lure is too large. As we change it leisurely for a smaller one of the same kind, the heavy plunge of a fish draws your attention up-stream, where a salmon is jumping repeatedly high out of water just below the

"A salmon springs out"

falls. "What is he jumping there for?" You will laugh when I tell you that he is trying to get a good look at the falls; but that is true, nevertheless. Come up to the fallen spruce that bridges the river, and let us watch him there for a while. Our big salmon will keep; he is in a rising mood; when we get him, fishing is over for the day for we have enough.

Below the falls, which are here some ten or twelve feet high, salmon are jumping continually. As you watch the heavy white rush of water other salmon poke their heads out of the foam, look at the falls a moment, and disappear. Then a silver gleam flashes through some black water; a salmon springs out, flies in a great arc up to the rim of the falls, just touches the falling sheet of water, plunges over the brim, and disappears with a victorious flash of his broad tail into the swift water above. He has done it— jumped the falls,—and though the whole thing was swift as light, you have the impression that at last you know just how it was done.

Down yonder are some lower falls, and there you can see the salmon leaping clear over them in a single spring, rising out of the foam below and disappearing into the swift, clear stream above, without even touching the falling sheet of water; but here it is different. Salmon after salmon springs out, lands on his tail against the falling water just below the brim of the falls, and then plunges up and over, as his tail, like a bent spring, recoils from under him.

Now throw a stone or two into the falls, just where that last salmon struck. There! you hit it with a big one; and in a flash you see and hear that the sheet of falling water is thinnest there, and that the face of the rock lies close beneath. Here is a suggestion which may explain why and how the salmon jump.

Down on the still reaches of the river they jump continually, especially in the late afternoon. That is partly for fun and play, no doubt; but it is also for practice, to accustom themselves to high jumps, and to learn how to land on head or tail as they please. Here under the falls they jump out of water, and again hold their heads above the foam, as you see them, to study the place and see where they must strike in order to succeed. There to the left is a spot where the falls are a foot lower than the average; but though you watch all clay you will not see a single salmon jump there, where you would naturally expect him to try. The river pours swiftly through this notch, worn in the softer rock, and spurts far out from the face of the wall beneath. Were a salmon to strike there, he would find no solid purchase from which to finish his leap, but would be overwhelmed in a flash by the force of the cataract.

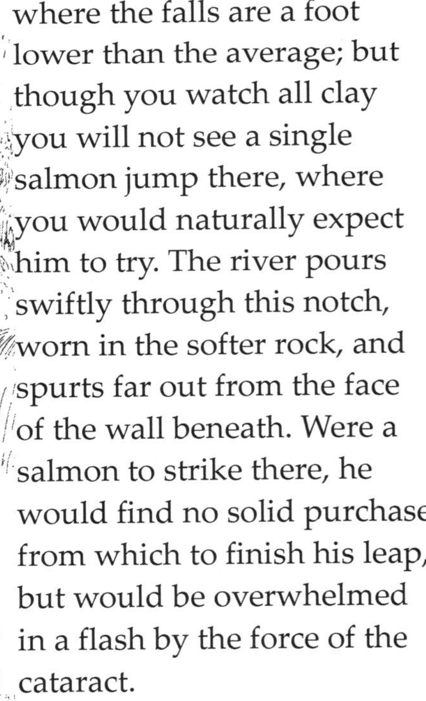

To the right of this notch are two places which seem to be favorites with the salmon. Again and again, in days of watching, you will see them land on their bent tails in these two spots. As they land their tails strike down through the falling water, touch the rock beneath, and recoil like steel springs; and the salmon bound up, like rubber balls, and vanish over the brim. Occasionally they fail, and you have a confused impression of a big silver fish hurled into the turmoil below. Look ! there in the shallow eddy, beside that rock on the shore. There is a fat, eighteen-pound salmon struggling to hold his place. The cruel gash in his side shows all too plainly that he failed in his jump and was hurled back upon the rocks.

To stay here now is death to Kopseep; for even should he escape the bear and otter and eagle, a multitude of parasites, plant and animal, would fasten upon the wound and suck his life away. That is what his slime is for, to oil his silver sides and keep away these deadly fungi that swarm in fresh water. Once the scales are scraped away and the tender flesh laid bare Kopseep has no protection, and to stay in the river is suicide. But even here Nature is not unkind; nor does she ever forget a creature's needs. Other salmon eat nothing while they are moving up the rivers to their spawning beds, and appetite itself vanishes; but the wounded fish there suddenly feels within him the need of recuperation, and takes to feeding greedily upon whatever the river brings him. Toss in a worm, a bit of meat, a fly,—anything eatable, and he rises to it swiftly. In a few hours he feels better, and whirls in the current and goes speeding back to the sea, where the salt water destroys the parasites and heals his wound and makes him strong again. But he will not come back to the river again this year.

A half-mile above there is another fall, higher than this one. Let us go up, and find there the most difficult problem of all to answer.

A single glance at the falls tells you instantly that they are too high for any salmon to leap. Other rivers with a fall no higher than this one are barred to the salmon, which run up only as far as the falls and then turn back to the sea, or else spawn at the mouths of shallow brooks along the way. But the salmon in this river go clear to the head waters. You can see them jumping and catch a dozen above the falls. Here, just below the cataract, they are springing high out of water, or poking their heads out of the foam, just as they did at the lower falls, in order to study the difficult place.

As you watch, a big salmon flashes up in a great arc and tumbles into the sheet of falling water, not half-way up to the top. Soon another follows him, striking in the same place. You watch closely but see nothing more; they have simply vanished into the falls. A dead salmon floats past you; another is gasping in a shallow eddy; a third lies half eaten by an otter under the shelving bank. Here is a place, evidently, where many fail. Now watch the topmost rim of the waterfall.

Ten minutes pass slowly while you keep your eyes on the line where the yellow flood breaks over the brim of the falls. There! a flash of living silver breaks the uneven line; a broad tail cuts the air in a curving sweep as a salmon plunges safely over the top into the swift water above. That is probably the fish that you saw vanish into the falls, ten feet below. Now we must follow him, if we are to learn anything more of his methods.

For twenty years—ever since I first fished the Saevogle—I had wondered how it was possible for salmon to get up a waterfall which was plainly impossible to leap; and on reading the books I found that almost every salmon fisherman for two centuries had puzzled over the same problem. Standing under these falls, one day, and throwing stones at the spots in the falling sheet of water where the salmon were plunging in, it occurred to me suddenly that it might be possible to go in myself and find out what they were doing. On two rivers I had tried it unsuccessfully, and though I had glimpses of salmon lying on the wet rocks inside the falls, I was almost swept away in the cataract. Here the task proved unexpectedly easy; for on one side the swift flood shot far out from the face of the rock, and the falling sheet of water was not heavy enough to knock one off his feet. So, if you don't mind a soaking,—which will do no harm here in the deep wilderness, where there are no microbes to give you a cold,—let us after our salmon.

With rubber coats falling down over waders, we slip through and under the edge of the broad sheet of falling water and stand close against the rocky wall. It is cool and wet here; the hollows in the rough face of the rock arc brimming over; the air is full of heavy mist; but the flood pours over our heads without touching us. A salmon is kicking violently among the stones, and you brush him with your foot out into the cataract. As we move along to the middle of the stream, pressing close against the wall, with the thunder of the falls pouring over us harmlessly, we come suddenly upon salmon everywhere: on the stones, in deep hollows of the rock, struggling up the scarred and pitted face of the cliff itself. Push on a little farther, and now you see a great crevice slanting diagonally up the wall almost to the brim of the fall over your head. A thin stream of water runs through it, making a fall within a fall. This crevice is full of salmon; some dead, some lying and resting quietly in the hollows, others kicking, flapping, sliding upward over the wet stone and the slippery bodies of their fellows to the life above.

Your first visit may solve the problem, for this river at least; or you may have to return again and again before you see the thing accomplished from beginning to end. This is the time, for the river is just beginning to rise after the rains, and great runs of salmon are moving up from the pools below; while those that were here, resting below the falls for the great effort, feel the onward movement and start upward to the spawning-grounds at the head of the river.

Where the Salmon Jump

As you stand here salmon after salmon comes flying in through the falling sheet of white water. Some strike fair against the wall, rebound, and are swept away like smoke; others, as if they knew the spot, plunge into a wet hollow, rest an instant from the shock, then wriggle and leap to the hollows above. Here is one that dashes in and lights fairly in the great crevice at your shoulder, on the bodies of three or four other salmon that are lying there gasping and struggling feebly. In an instant his broad tail is threshing violently, pushing him upward in desperate flappings and wrigglings, up over the rock, over the bodies of his fellows; resting here, leaping boldly there over a little ridge, up and up, till with one last effort he plunges over the brim and is gone.

However it may be on other rivers, the problem here is an amazingly simple one. The salmon simply leap into the falls, trusting to luck or instinct, or more probably to knowledge gained from previous experience, to break through the sheet of falling water and land in one of the numerous hollows or crevices in the face of the rock. Then, if not stunned or swept away in the first effort, they struggle up the side of the rock itself, and over the bodies of their less successful fellows, till near enough to the top to leap over.

Here, as indeed in most falls, one may notice a curious rhythmic movement of the water. It rarely pours over the falls in an even flood, but rather in a succession of spurts, with slower and lighter movements between; so that, both by eye and ear, one gets the impression of throbbing in the water's movement, as if the river were only one of many arteries, and somewhere behind them all a great heart were beating and driving the waters onward in slow, regular, mighty pulsations. Undoubtedly the salmon make use of this fact, resting near the top of the rock for a slower and lighter movement of the water, when they throw themselves over the brim of the falls and so avoid being swept away after accomplishing the most difficult and dangerous part of their journey.

Desperate as it is, this is probably the method used on other rivers where salmon surmount a waterfall which is plainly too high to leap. Dr. Elwood Worcester, of Boston, writes me that while salmon fishing on White Bay his guides told, him of a place where the salmon climbed the cliff behind a fall, and where the fishermen collected barrels of fish for winter use every season. He went with them behind the fall, and watched for hours as the salmon plunged in and then began the almost impossible task of leaping up the rock. There, as here, only a fraction of the struggling fish ever reached the top. Some of the unsuccessful ones tried again; others sped away to heal their wounds; the rest lay quiet among the rocks awaiting the poor fishermen, or floated away to feed the mink and the eagle. Nature called the many in order to choose a few, and the whole process was accompanied by that apparent waste and perfect economy with which Nature always accomplishes her object.

As we go down-stream and take up our position on the flat rock again, a heavy plunge out on the edge of the white current shows that our big salmon is still there and in a rising mood. He will take our fly now; and the rest is a matter of skill, with a large element of luck, which is all in the salmon's favor. But our glimpse under the falls has aroused a new interest in the hidden life of the big fish, resting and playing there in the turmoil; so let us hear his story before we catch him.

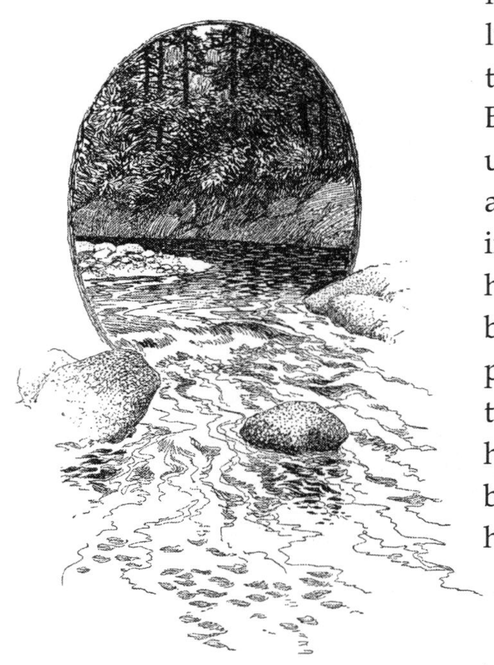

THE STORY
OF KOPSEEP

The Story of Kopseep

ONE late autumn, a few years ago, a big salmon came up to the head waters of the river and sought out a place for herself where she might hide her eggs. All summer long she had journeyed slowly up the river, resting below the falls and rapids to gather her strength, and choosing the bright moonlit nights to hurry up through the riffles, where Mooween the bear was waiting to catch her as she passed. Now, with most of the danger and all the effort behind her, she came straight to the shallows at the mouth of a cold brook where the bottom was covered with sand and yellow pebbles. Where the current rippled evenly over its bed of golden gravel she found the place she was seeking, and like fish-hawks returning in the spring, her first care was to repair the nest that had been used for centuries by other salmon. Her broad tail fanned away the coating of mud that had settled over the pebbles, and the current swept it away downstream. Bits of rotten wood and twigs and leaves that had jammed among the stones she took up in her mouth and carried to one side, leaving the rest all white and clean. As she worked a great male fish, with a kipper hook on his lower jaw, came surging up and chose her for his mate, and then began circling about her, fighting the other salmon and chasing away the trout that swarmed hungrily about, waiting for the feast of salmon eggs that was to follow.

When the nest was at last ready, the big male fish came and plowed long furrows through it with the beak that had been growing on the point of his lower jaw for this purpose ever since he entered fresh water. These furrows were fanned clean with tails and fins, and then his mate settling upon the nest began depositing her eggs, thousands and thousands of them; so many that, had they all hatched and grown, the river must have been full of salmon.

That was a busy time for the old male with the hooked jaw. As the eggs were laid he covered them hurriedly with gravel to keep the current

from washing them away, and to hide them from the little trout and parrs that flashed about like sunbeams, and that, spite of his fierce snaps and rushes, would dart in to grab a mouthful and scud away to eat it under the banks or stones where he could not follow them. At times the little bandits seemed to hunt in packs, like wolves; and while the big salmon was chasing one of their number, the others would flash in and gobble up all the uncovered tidbits. They would even steal under the mother salmon and snatch away eggs as they were laid, till the old male came surging back and scattered them a puff of smoke into their unseen dens.

At last, however, the eggs were all laid, and covered up safely where even the parrs could not find them; and spite of all losses, there were thousands enough left in every nest to warrant a full supply of young salmon. Then scores of the great fish, which had grown lank and clingy and faint from their five months' fast and their tremendous efforts in running up the river, rested awhile, lying like logs over all the shallows, until the nights grew intensely still and over the quiet pools the ice began to tinkle its winter warning. A subtle command ran along the river, which our salmon, like all other fish, seemed to obey without knowing why or how they did so. One morning they all turned in the current at the same moment and went speeding back to the sea, leaving to the little brook the task of hatching their offspring. And the little brook, which was used to such things,

at once took up the work, singing to itself the same glad little song that it had crooned for a thousand years over the hidden cradles of all the young salmon it had ever brooded.

The winter passed slowly; a current of fresh water passed continually over the hidden treasures; and when the ice broke up in the spring there was a general breaking up down among the eggs in the gravel nest. Something stirred vigorously within an egg lodged between two white pebbles; the covering broke and out glided Kopseep, a tiny male salmon. Beginning his life with hunger, he had first eaten all that was left in the egg besides himself, and was nibbling at the shell when it broke and let him out. In an instant, following his instinct, he had settled in the tiny eddy behind one of the pebbles that had sheltered him. As the egg covering wavered on his tail he whirled like a wink and swallowed it. Then he settled behind his pebble again and took his first look at the world.

All around him the tiny salmon were making their way out of the nest. As they emerged the current seemed to sweep them away like mist; but in reality each one darted for the nearest stone or cover, and vanished as if the bed of the river had opened to swallow him. Quick

as they were, a score of them were seized by the hungry little trout and parrs that swarmed in the shallows, each one hiding under a stone and watching like a hawk for food. But Kopseep was safe under a root, whither he had darted from the shelter of his first pebble, and his struggle with the world had begun.

For a year he lived in the shallows as a little parr, hiding from his enemies and eating of the insect life that swarmed in the water. Then, as he grew in strength and quickness, he took to chasing and catching the tiny eels that squirmed in the mud under the still reaches of the brook, and would flash up from the bottom and out into the sunshine to catch and pull down a passing fly. After every sortie he would whirl and dart like a sunbeam under his root again. No need to look for enemies; they were all about him, and he always took it for granted that they were waiting to catch him, and that his safety lay in getting back to the cover of his own den before they had noticed his movements.

Occasionally, spite of his lightning dash, a little trout would spy him and dart between him and his sheltering root; and then Kopseep would make use of a trick which every little salmon seems to know by instinct. He would dart away, with the troutlet after him, to where the bottom was softest and whirl up a muddy cloud into which his enemy dashed headlong. Then, before the troutlet could find him,

Kopseep was hidden under an inch of soft mud; or else, fearing the big eels, he would scoot back under cover of the muddy screen to his own root, whither no enemy ever followed him.

As for the troutlet, he had speedily his own troubles to attend to. Besides the larger fish, which always chased all smaller ones that dared show themselves in open water, the mink was gliding in and out like a shadow. Kingfishers dropped in like plummets, getting a fish at almost every plunge; and the sheldrakes, that had a nest just above, were frightfully destructive, eating scores of trout in every day's fishing. So the troutlet, after one confused instant in the mud cloud, would forget our little samlet and flash away to his own den, thankful if he had himself escaped being seen and chased while he was chasing somebody else.

In the midst of all these clangers the parr lived and throve mightily, and if one can judge from his play,—for he had already begun to leap out of still water and tumble back with resounding splash in the quiet afternoons,—he reveled in the strength and gladness of life and in the abundance of good things to be had for the chasing. In his first autumn the big salmon appeared again in the shallows to spawn, and Kopseep joined

his fellows in scooting about and stealing the eggs whenever the big male with the hooked jaw was occupied in covering the furrows or chasing away the horde of active little robbers that swarmed about him.

Kopseep was now nearly six inches long, having increased a hundredfold in weight in a few months. Catching a glimpse of him as he flung himself out of water in vigorous play, you would have seen a beautiful little creature, his eyes bright as stars, his gleaming sides sprinkled with bright vermilion spots and crossed with the dark blue bars or finger-marks which indicate the parr state, and with exquisite pearly shells covering the deep red gills on either side. A trout, you might have said, as he rose like a flash to your fly; but another look would have told you plainly that he was more graceful and powerful, and likewise much more beautiful, than any trout that ever came out of the water.

All winter long he lay by his den, seeking little food and growing strangely lazy. When spring came a curious change crept over him. When he ventured into still water and looked in the wonderful mirror

there (which was the under surface of the pool, and which you can see yourself by looking up obliquely into a glass of water), he saw that all his beautiful blue bars and vermilion spots were slowly disappearing, being covered up by a new growth of silver scales. By the middle of May the new scales had covered all his body. A curious uneasiness filled him as Nature whispered that the new suit she had given him was for a new life, and at the word Kopseep turned tail to the current and went speeding down the river, where he had never been before. He was a smolt now, and all his brothers from the same nest were speeding down the river with him, leaving their sisters, still in their bright parr coats, playing and feeding about the shallows where they were born.

It was a wonderful journey for our little smolt, —the more so because he had never before ventured away from the home brook, and he knew not why he went nor whither he was going on the long rushing migration. Down, down he hurried, now shooting easily through the dancing riffles, now whirled along the rush and tumble of a boiling rapid, and now caught up with irresistible force and hurled outward into a white chaos where all his universe seemed to be falling blindly into space that roared and trembled beneath him. But always his first instinct to keep close to bottom was with him, and even in the worst of rapids a turn of his tail would send him down to where the water eddied and rolled leisurely among the stones, while the rush and uproar went on harmlessly overhead. And everywhere he went he had a sense of comradeship, of hosts that were moving onward with him to the same end; for the river was full of smolts, gliding, dodging, flashing like silver everywhere in the cool dark eddies, and all moving swiftly downward to the sea.

So they passed from the hills to the low marsh lands and lakes; and here they met shoals of great silver fish, their own mothers, beginning their long journey upward to the shallows which the smolts had just left behind them.

A new flavor came into the water as they followed the slow current. It was the taste of the sea, and a great thrill and tingle passed through the shoal of smolts, making them leap for joy and dash onward, down through the first gentle surges of the tide, down faster and faster, till they scattered suddenly and hid as another shoal of great salmon flashed into sight, with a score of seals darting and twisting after them like so many black demons. Over the hidden smolts passed the chase, like the rush of a tornado; then the little fellows darted out of their hiding and quivered onward till they passed deep under the

surge and thunder of the breakers and vanished into the cool green forests of kelp and seaweed that waved their soft arms everywhere on the ocean's floor, beckoning the frightened little wanderers to rest and safety.

Here they waited a few days and fed abundantly, and looked out with wonder from their green coverts, as from a window, at the strange new life that passed by them,—hermit-crabs and starfish and sea-robins and skates and stingarees and lobsters and dolphins and Peter Grunters,—all with some outlandish peculiarity, or some queer, crazy way of flitting about, like dwarfs or hobgoblins; so that every day Wonderland itself seemed to pass in procession before their windows. But the fever of migration was still upon them, and soon the shoal was moving onward more eagerly than before.

New dangers met them with every mile. Strange and savage monsters with goggle eyes and stickle backs and huge gaping mouths surged out at them from coverts of rock and kale and sea-moss; and from the bottom itself, where they looked like bits of innocent mud, flatfish and flounders leaped up into the very midst of the passing shoal. But their life in the quick waters of the brooks had made these little smolts like bundles of tempered steel springs. They were quicker far than the big savage bandits that looked so much more dangerous than they really were; and our own little smolt found no difficulty in dodging them and hiding under a frond of kelp till they had surged by. So the shoal passed on, still following the almost imperceptible flavor of their own river, till they were nearly twenty miles out at sea, and up from the bottom rose a ridge of rocky hills covered with waving sea growth. Here the fever suddenly left them and the shoal scattered, each to his own little den, just as they had done in the shallows far away in the green wilderness.

A new and wonderful life had begun for Kopseep, and the very best thing about it was the abundance of good things to eat. Millions of minute *Crustacea,* tender and delicious, would swarm at times over his den, filling the water full of food and coloring it bright pink, like a tomato soup. He had only to swim lazily through it once or twice with his mouth open and come back gorged to his den, as if he had been swimming around in a rich pudding. In an hour he was hungry and would roll up through his strange food bath, filling himself again and again till the swarm passed on with the tides. Then, led by his perpetual hunger, he passed over the rocky ridge to where the ocean's floor slanted upward and spread out into broad level plains. Here the cod had laid their eggs in uncounted millions, and the codlings covered the place like flies on a butcher's block. The little gourmand would stuff himself till the tails stuck out of his mouth; then with a wriggle he would spew them out and begin all over again, just for the delight of eating.

Naturally, with all this good feeding, Kopseep grew till his skin almost cracked to cover him. When he first came to the ocean he was hardly as long as your hand, and would weigh perhaps three ounces. In a month he was a strong, shapely fish, a foot long and weighing over a pound; and his appetite, instead of diminishing, only grew more and more voracious as he increased in weight. No more *Crustacea* or codlings for him now; he had himself joined the bandits that had at first frightened him, and was too big to be satisfied with such small fry. But when the shoals of brilliant caplin passed over him, making the sea look as if a rainbow had broken into bits and fallen there, his silver sides were seen flashing in and out among them. And then, as he grew bigger and the caplin passed on shoreward with the tides, the herring came drifting in, like great silver clouds, with the sea-birds screaming over them; and these were the best food of all.

So three months passed in the ocean and our little smolt had now become a grilse, or "gilsie," a beautiful fish of four pounds weight, with his silver sides spotted like a trout; only the spots were large and black instead of being small and red. As the summer waned scores of small salmon began to move uneasily along the rocky ridges where the grilse were hiding. A fever seemed to spread through the water, and salmon and grilse alike stopped their ravenous feeding. One morning the salmon moved off together, as if at command, and Kopseep with hundreds of his fellow-grilse followed them, the fever of motion growing stronger and stronger as they followed up the well-known flavor of their own river.

Near the shore they stopped for a few days, waiting for the tides of full moon; and old Daddy Crummet, who for weeks had not seen a salmon, set his nets again and found them each morning full to overflowing. Then when the tide was highest the shoal surged into the river's mouth, past the rocky point where the seals were waiting and barking like hungry dogs at the smell of meat.

With a rush our grilse shot past the point, where the water boiled and flashed as the shoal doubled away from their savage enemies. A lively young seal plunged after Kopseep; but the grilse was too quick, and the seal turned aside after a large and lazier fish. So he gained the fresh, water safely, and journeyed swiftly upward through the lakes, jumping

and playing in his strength, till he came to the first swift run of water below the little falls. Here he put his nose down in an eddy behind a sunken rock, and caught the current on his fins and tail in such a way as to hold himself in place without conscious effort, resting for his first leap and for the hard rush through the rapids above the falls.

While he waited here Kopseep felt his stomach shrinking within him. There were fish in the river,—minnows and trout and eels, and lazy chub that the mink and fishhawk were catching,—but Kopseep watched them indifferently and suffered them to go their own ways unmolested. Strangely enough all his voracious appetite of the past few months had left him—and lucky it was too; for otherwise a single run of salmon would destroy every trout and frog and little fish in the river. And that is perhaps why Nature takes away the salmon's appetite and keeps it for him all the while that he is going on a journey in fresh water.

As he lay in his eddy resting, or playing with any bright-colored thing that the current brought him, a troop of little silver smolts went hurrying and

flashing by on their way to the sea. Though he knew it not, they were the little sisters that he had left as parr in the shallows when he went away, four months ago. No wonder Kopseep did not recognize them; for they were hardly as big as the caplin that he had been eating by scores for weeks past. He watched them curiously as they darted past, wondering where they came from and why they hurried so; then he moved up under the falls and began to jump and poke his head out of the foam to study the place, as the salmon were doing, before he took his leap.

He tried it at last: flung himself headlong into the falls and was promptly knocked end over end, and in a wink found himself bruised and quivering back by his own rock again. That seemed to teach him wisdom; for at the next attempt he shot through a black eddy from which all the salmon took their leap, flung himself upward in a glorious arc, struck fair in the swift water above the falls, and in an instant was flashing and plunging up through the rapids. Not till he reached a great pool two or three miles above did he halt, and then he settled down in another eddy to rest for his next effort.

So he journeyed upwards for nearly two months, tarrying below the worst rapids for a fall of water, and waiting for the rains wherever the river spread into broad shallows that hardly covered the salmon as they wriggled and splashed their way upward. Here, one moonlit night, something like a black stump stood squarely athwart Kopseep's path. He was splashing his way toward it when a sudden alarm made him halt behind a rock. A heedless fat salmon went lumbering by; the stump suddenly started into life; then the fat salmon went flying out on shore from the sweep of a paw, and Mooween the bear went humping and jumping after him to catch him before he could, scramble back into the river.

That was enough for our grilse. Ever afterwards when he saw, on moonlit nights, a black rock or stump in the shallows, he watched awhile to see if it moved, before going through the dangerous place. And this is the test which all salmon and trout apply to every suspicious object: if it moves, it is dangerous, whether on land or water. That is why you catch only flashing glimpses of them as you walk along the bank; while on the other hand, if you sit very still on a rock in the salmon pool and trail your toe or finger or a single leaf in the current, you may see a big salmon move up to examine it leisurely; and sometimes

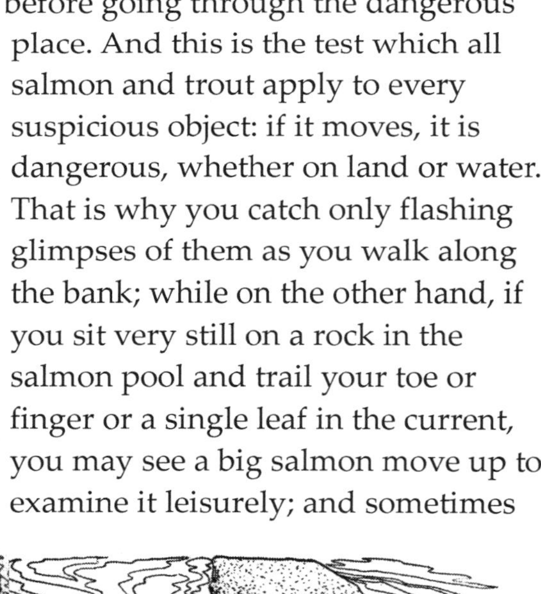

he will spatter water all over you as he plunges at the object in play and whirls back to his eddy again.

Late in October Kopseep found himself once more on the shallows at the mouth of the brook where he was born. He went straight to the root under which he used to hide; but the familiar place was grown so small that his head would not go into it; and the eddy there that used to hold him securely was now of no consequence whatever. So he took to cruising leisurely around the tiny world that had once seemed to him so big and full of danger. Danger? why, this was a place of absolute peace compared with the dragon-haunted green forests under the sea. He was so big now that—

A thrill tingled all through Kopseep as he darted aside, making the shallow water roll and bubble, and whirled and doubled madly, and flashed in and out of the startled river with a long, black, snaky wake doubling after him, as if it were his own shadow that he was trying to escape. Like a flash he rose and leaped back, a clear eight feet, over the shadow, which doubled swiftly and seized another grilse that was plowing furrows in a gravel nest. Out of the troubled waters slid first the head, then the long back and tail of an otter, which climbed the bank and stood mewing over her catch. Two more shadows glided into the river at her call, making our grilse jump and flash away and hide again; but the new-comers were only two otter cubs that as yet had learned to catch only stupid chub and suckers. In a moment they were out on the bank, crouched with their long backs arched like frightened cats, nibbling daintily at the salmon; while Kopseep, forgetting all about them, roamed boldly over the shallows, looking for a little salmon to be his mate.

He found her at last, preparing her nest just below the mouth of the brook, and began circling watchfully about her. Other grilse were numerous, and in searching for a mate they would enter his circle aggressively, as if it were a chip that Kopseep was carrying on his shoulder. Like a flash he would rush at them, lock jaws, and tug and push and bully them out of the circle. Then, when he returned, he had to bite and gouge and drive away the sea-trout—huge fellows, some of them, as big as himself—that swarmed hungrily about, waiting for the feast of salmon eggs.

It was late autumn; the banks were strangely still and white, and ice had formed over all the still pools when Kopseep turned downstream again, leaving the eggs of his mate safely covered in the new nest. He was like a kelt, or black salmon, now,—that is, a dark fish that has grown thin and hungry from tarrying and fasting too long in fresh water. Down he went, through the rapids and over the falls, in a desperate hurry that made him speed faster than the swift river, which had seemed so wonderful on his first journey in the springtime. In a single day's racing he covered the entire distance, snapping up every little fish that crossed his swift path, and the next day found him back in his den in the rocky ridge under the ocean. This was the salmon's own foraging ground; and among the multitudes that swarmed there Kopseep saw numerous fat young grilse, almost as big as himself; but he knew not that these were the same little sisters that he had met coming down, and that had changed rapidly from smolt to grilse while he was fighting his hard way up the river.

The few rare fishermen who visit this part of the coast wonder why in this river—and indeed in many others—they catch only male grilse; but the reason is probably a very simple one. The females pass the grilse state in the ocean, growing steadily until the following spring, when males and females enter the river together as fully developed salmon of eight or ten pounds' weight.

All winter long our young grilse, famished by his long fasting, gorged himself and grew fat and doubled his weight. When the May moon drew near her full the migratory fever again ran along the rocky ridge under the ocean; for even down there, in the cold green underworld, Nature comes with the same message that sets the buds to swelling and the birds to singing. The largest salmon felt it first and drifted away in a dense shoal, following up the delicate flavor of their own river as a dog follows an air scent, or else remembering, as a mule does, every turn and winding of the trail that has once been followed. A month later Kopseep, with hundreds of his fellows, moved leisurely away after them.

He was a salmon now, and had to take his chances with the seals that watched on the point of rocks and that neglected all other fish when the first run of salmon came plunging in through the breakers. He had passed them safely, after a lively chase, and was playing and jumping hilariously in the pool at the head of the first lake, when a curious accident sent him hurrying back to the sea. And that was only the beginning of a long chain of causes which made him bigger than all his fellows.

On the lake were a pair of loons that had a nest on a bog hard by, and that were always fishing. Hukweem was deep under water chasing a big trout, one day, which darted into Kopseep's pool and vanished under a root. As Hukweem sped noiselessly by, trailing a great string of silver bubbles, the waving of a great tail caught his eye just beyond the root, and like a flash he plunged at it, driving his pointed bill deep into Kopseep's side. Had it been a big trout the blow would have stunned him on the spot; but at the first touch the salmon tore himself free and leaped clear of the water. Hukweem passed on, seeing his mistake, and the next moment Kopseep was back in the pool, fanning the water quietly as if nothing whatever had happened.

Since entering fresh water Kopseep's appetite had vanished; but now it began suddenly to gnaw again. That was simply Nature's way of telling him to go back to the sea, where he might be healed. It was not the pain of his wound; for, like other fish, he seemed to feel nothing of that kind. Had he stayed in the fresh water the parasites would speedily have fastened on the raw flesh and killed him; but of that he knew nothing. He simply felt hungry, and remembered that in the sea there was food in abundance. Salmon fishermen have always noticed how wounded fish suddenly begin feeding.

Sometimes when the wound is no more than the mark of a net, which has split a fin or brushed off a ring of scales around the head, the marked salmon will plunge at a fly more vigorously than any of his fellows in the pool, and will even take worms or a shiner, if your sportmanship allow you to offer them. So Kopseep, feeling only the hunger,—which was Nature's simple direction, without her explanations,—turned swiftly back to the sea, and almost within the hour was resting in his old den under the rocks again.

Here he stayed all summer long. While other salmon moved off in successive shoals and battled their way up the river, Kopseep, whose migratory fever seemed to be cured by the thrust of a loon's bill, gave himself up to the unlimited abundance of the ocean, and discovered for himself, one day, a new and delicious food supply. It was late in the summer, after the caplin had passed by, and Kopseep, after his wont, was gliding in and out of the green forest arches and poking his hungry nose into every den among the rocks. In a little arched doorway with some waving green weeds for a curtain his nose touched something soft, which instantly shrank back closer to the sheltering rock. Kopseep pulled it out promptly and found a small lobster, which was hiding there waiting for his new shell to grow. A delicious taste, the most wonderful he had ever experienced, filled his mouth as he bolted the morsel. All excitement, after the manner of feeding fish, Kopseep put his nose into another den and found another lobster, a bigger one, that offered no resistance as he was dragged out and eaten.

It was all so different from previous experience that the salmon knew not what to make of it. He had often passed lobsters before, crawling slowly along the bottom on the tiptoes of their queer legs, or shooting backward like winks and hiding in the mud when frightened by a huge and hungry sea-bass. Their shells were too hard for Kopseep to think of cracking; and besides, each lobster carried two pairs of big ugly jaws in front of him as he yew-yawed along. These jaws were always wide open,—one pair armed with little teeth for catching and holding things, and the other with big teeth for crushing whatever was caught. So Kopseep had wisely let the lobsters alone, and had no idea that they were good to eat. Now, however, the hard shells had all split along the backs, and the lobsters left the shoal water and the fishermen's lobster-pots to seek out deep hidden caves among the rocks. There they crawled out of the old shells and lay very quiet in hiding, waiting for the new shells to grow hard enough to make it safe for them to venture into the world once more.

It was at this very time, when the lobsters were most defenseless, that Kopseep found them. There were hundreds of them, from the size of your hand up to the big, shy fellow that would fill a basket, each one hidden away in his own den; and Kopseep left all other game and took to lobster hunting. It was a tingling kind of sport, gliding noiselessly with every sense on the alert through the waving forests and over the rocks; for scores of hungry bandits — monstrous sea-bass and horse-mackerel and, worst of all, dogfish—had taken advantage of the new food supply and were lurking in every covert, ready to snap up the salmon and other fish that came hunting for lobsters. So Kopseep never knew, when he approached a den, whether he would find a tidbit for himself or an ogre to eat him up; and his hunting was very much as if you were prowling among the woods and mountain caves, expecting game every moment, but not knowing whether you would find a rabbit that you wanted, or a big grizzly bear or a dragon that might want you.

His method of hunting here never varied. He would glide among the waving green fronds, trying, as every other wild creature does, to see everything without himself being seen, until he spied a little cave or den that might hide a soft-shelled lobster. Then he would settle down where the sea growth hid him and watch all the surroundings steadily. If nothing stirred, and if no suspicious glint of bronze or silver scales flickered in the waving forest, he would glide up and peer into the den. If the lobster were there, and not too big, he dragged him out and ate him quickly; but at the first suspicious glint or movement he would whirl like a flash, making the delicate seaweeds roll and quiver violently to hide his flight, and the next instant he was fifty feet away and hidden so cunningly that the big shark or sea-bass would drive straight over his head without seeing him.

Once, as he hunted in this way, he spied a queer cave in the rocks with gleaming white points reaching up from the bottom and down from the top, like stalactites and stalagmites, and with just room enough for him to swim in between them,—a perfect place, it looked, for a nice soft lobster to be hiding. Kopseep lay in the weeds and watched a few moments, then glided forward to enter. Just then something began to glow dull red over the cave; and in a flash Kopseep had whirled away, while the long weeds swayed and rolled and hid him as he darted aside. In a moment he was stealing back to watch the den from another hiding-place. Suddenly the whole cave seemed to move and tremble. The white points above and below came slowly together, and there was no more an open doorway. Out from the rocks glided a queer monster of a mouthfish, colored like the gray rocks, with dull red eyes and a head like a Chinese dragon. He looked around for a moment, backed into his lair, opened his huge mouth,—and there was the cave again, looking just like a den in the rocks. But Kopseep was not looking for any more lobsters in that neighborhood, and he was a wiser and more wary fish as he glided away on his solitary hunting.

So the long summer passed by, and Kopseep grew daily larger with his comfortable and lazy living. When his brothers and sisters came down from the river they found him more than twice their size and a full twenty pounds in weight. By spring he had added five pounds more, and when the first shoal of big salmon moved riverward with the tides of full moon Kopseep was among them. For on this run, when the river is full and strong with the spring floods, only the largest fish are equal to the hard work of climbing the falls and rapids.

So the years went by with little change in Kopseep's methods of living. Only he grew bigger and bigger, and his long summer in the sea had made him even more full of moods and whims than most salmon. Once, when a flood had blocked the river with logs, so that the salmon could neither swim under nor jump over the obstacle, he had gone down the coast with a few of his fellows and run up a new stream, contrary to the habits of all salmon, which in general run up only the rivers in which they are born. Another season, when he was heavier and lazier than usual, he had ascended the river only as far as the first rapids, just above tide-water. There, with a dozen unusually large fish, he spent a month playing idly and sleeping, as salmon often do. And when you hooked one of these big fellows he bolted headlong down the river, and either smashed your tackle, or, if you were quick enough to leap into your canoe—for they never stopped or sulked like other salmon—he took you swiftly out through the breakers, and you had the rare experience of playing a salmon in the open sea.

This year Kopseep has come up leisurely as far as the pool below the falls; and this is as far as he will ever get, if our tackle holds and he still keeps on rising at pretty things that the current sweeps over him. See ! there he is, a monster salmon, plunging out of the white rips, just where we left him when we sat down by the river to hear his story.

We have "rested" him long enough now, and have changed the number-six Jock Scott to a number-eight of the same kind; and all the while Kopseep is rising splendidly. A subtile excitement creeps over you as the long line shoots out from the springing tip, farther and farther, till it falls straight across the white turmoil below which the salmon is lying. Swiftly the leader swings down and straightens in the current; the tiny fly whirls up and dances for an instant in the very spot where you saw Kopseep's rise. There ! a swift rush, the flash of heavy shoulders as he turns downward. Don't strike now, as you would a trout; for the spring of your tip against the heavy plunge of that big fish snap your leader as if it were made cobweb. A ponderous surge at the end of your rod, a light pull to set the hook fast; then your heart jumps to your mouth, and all your nerves thrill and tingle and shout hilariously as your reel screams at the first terrific rush. Out of the river springs a huge salmon, shooting up like a great jack-in-a-box, and tumbles in and jumps out again, here, there, everywhere at once, like a rooster with his head cut off. Away he goes, *zzzzim-m-m-m !* leaping clear and throwing himself broadside across ten feet of white water, shaking his head like a dog with a woodchuck; and then a headlong rush and tumble down the first rapids with the reel screaming shrill defiance after him at every plunge.

Noel has started to his feet at the first rush and reaches instinctively for the long gaff. " Py cosh ! oh, py cosh, beeg one ! " he says, staring open-mouthed at the torrent, not knowing where Kopseep will come up next. Then he settles back and fills his pipe, knowing well that a half-hour of delicate, skillful work must follow before you will get any glimpse of the big fish other than what he chooses to give you by leaping clear of the water, trying to strike the line with his tail, or to shake himself free of the tormenting little thing that plucks him by the jaw and that holds on spite of all his shaking and jumping.

He is down in the pool below now, resting for an instant in the eddy under a big rock. Three fourths of your line is already out of the reel, and if he makes another rush downstream you must lose him. Down you go, lively ! Scrambling over the rocks, floundering through the water, slipping, sliding, stumbling, clown you go; all the while with your rod up and bent to keep a strain on the fish, and with the reel singing its rhythmic *zum, zum, zum,* as you hurriedly gather in the line.

Get below your salmon now, and stay below him if you possibly can; for then he will have to fight against the current as well as against the spring of your rod. As you carry out the cunning maneuver Kopseep starts off in another series of wild leaps and rushes, swings wide across the river, and again darts below you. He lies quiet in one deep spot where the pull of your rod will just balance the push of the current. The line stands straight up, humming steadily, while a spurt of white water curls up beside it. All the while you feel a steady succession of harsh tugs and jerks that threaten every instant to part your tackle.

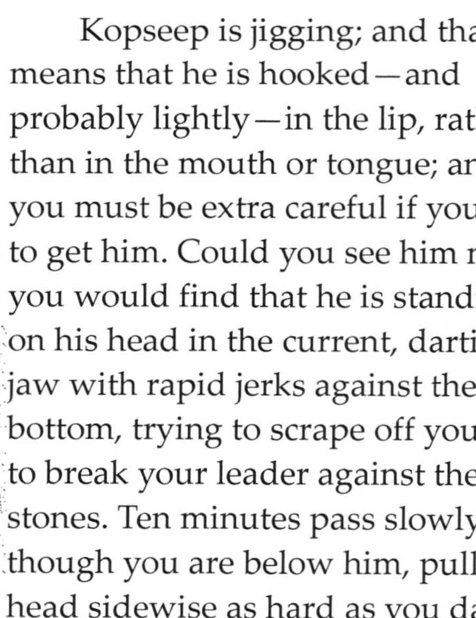

Kopseep is jigging; and that means that he is hooked—and probably lightly—in the lip, rather than in the mouth or tongue; and that you must be extra careful if you expect to get him. Could you see him now, you would find that he is standing fair on his head in the current, darting his jaw with rapid jerks against the bottom, trying to scrape off your fly or to break your leader against the stones. Ten minutes pass slowly, and though you are below him, pulling his head sidewise as hard as you dare, you have not budged him an inch. Then Noel appears, gliding in and out like a shadow among the trees on the bank.

"Some stones, Noel—big ones," you call to him; and the Indian begins to hurl stones at the spot where Kopseep is sulking. A lucky one starts him at last and he is off like a flash, rushing and jumping all over the pool; while you endeavor desperately to reel in the bagging line and to keep Kopseep out of the strong rush of water against the farther bank. Spite of you he surges into it; then, feeling the full power of the flood, he starts straight clown like an express train for the distant sea. After him you go, splashing like a startled moose through the pools, jumping the rocks like a goat, down, down through the rapids, with a heavy side pull—for you are getting desperate—at every turn of the river, till with a sigh of immense satisfaction you lead him out of the current into a still, deep reach of the river. And here the fight begins all over again.

Up to the present moment every chance in the unequal struggle was in the salmon's favor; but now you venture a wee, small hope that you may get him. Down below are some heavy rapids where you can neither follow nor hold your fish; so for half an hour you coax and humor and bully him, letting him have his own way when he is heading where you want him to go, but straining your light tackle to the breaking point to turn him away from the rapids. Then a great silver side rolls up heavily for an instant, showing that he is weary enough to be led, and you begin cautiously to reel him in to the bank.

Noel has disappeared, thinking, of course, that you lost your fish in the second desperate run through the rapids. You are half glad, for now you have a chance to land a salmon in the most sportsmanlike way of all, by beaching him yourself without help from the big gaff. There is only one possible spot hereabouts for so delicate a landing,—a little shingly beach where the bank shelves gently into the river. If you can lead him there on his side, at the first touch of the bottom he will flap his tail and kick himself out on land, aided by the gentle pull of your line. Just below the spot a broken stub leans far out, only two or three feet above the water. That is the danger point; but you must either risk it or shout for Noel, and you are glad, thinking of Kopseep, to give him the one small chance.

Now you avoid the beginner's eagerness and the mistake of being in too much of a hurry, and play your salmon till he rolls up on his side and lies there fanning the water; then gently, very gently, you lead him towards the shingle. He is almost yours; you could gaff him yourself as he swings past you, and your nerves tingle as you see how big he is. But at the first touch of the stones a new strength quivers suddenly in Kopseep. He turns on his belly, surges heavily down-stream, and spite of the straining rod passes slowly, powerfully under the leaning stub. You drop your rod instantly to the horizontal, so that your leader will not touch the wood, and draw him out towards the middle of the river. Again he rolls up on his side exhausted, and lies for a moment just below the stub. His eyes see it dimly, and with a last mighty effort he turns and leaps clear over it upstream. The line doubles around the log; he falls with all his weight on the taut leader; there is a heavy splash. Then the salmon is lying free in the shallows; the fly swings loose under the leaning stub with a tiny white bit of Kopseep's lip glistening on the barb.

On the instant you have dropped your rod, and all the sportsman's calm vanishes in the fisherman's eagerness as you jump forward to grab him. Your hands grip his broad back; but his slippery sides seem to ooze out between your fingers as he rolls away. A swift plunge as he sees his big enemy; then a broad tail waves triumphantly over the flood and the salmon vanishes into the deeps.

Good-by, Kopseep, and good luck ! You're the biggest fish I have seen all summer, and of course you got away. Up at Kopswaugan the salmon are still rising; but I have no more heart for the little nine-pounders. Till next summer then, when I shall look for you again in the same place under the falls. Meanwhile, may the bear and the seal and the shark and the net always miss you. The fisherman has no regrets that your story is not yet ended.

Cheokhes, *chē-ok-hĕs'* , the mink.
Cheplahgan, *chep-lâh'gan*, the bald eagle.
Ch'geegee-lokh-sis, *ch'gee-gee' lock-sis*, the chickadee.
Chigwooltz, *chig-wooltz'*, the bullfrog.
Clóte Scarpe, a legendary hero, like Hiawatha, of the Northern Indians. Pronounced variously, Clote Scarpe, Groscap, Gluscap, etc.
Commoosie, *com-moo-sie'*, a little shelter, or hut, of boughs and bark.
Deedeeaskh, *dee-dee' ask*, the blue jay.
Eleemos, *el-ee'mos*, the fox.
Hawahak, *hâ-wâ-hăk'*, the hawk.
Hetokh, *hĕt'ŏkh*, the deer.
Hukweem, *huk-weem'*, the great northern diver, or loon.
Ismaques, *iss-mâ-ques'*, the fish-hawk.
Kagax, *kăg'ăx*, the weasel.
Kakagos, *kâ-kâ-gŏs'*, the raven.
K'dunk, *k'dunk'*, the toad.
Keeokuskh, *kee-o-kusk'*, the muskrat.

Keeonekh, *kee'o-nek,* the otter.
Keesuolukh, *kee-su-ō'luk,* the Great Mystery, i.e. God.
Killooleet, *kil'loo-leet,* the white-throated sparrow.
Kookooskoos, *koo-koo-skoos',* the great horned owl.
Kopseep, *kop'seep,* the salmon.
Koskomenos, *kŏs' kŏm-e-nŏs',* the kingfisher.
Kupkawis, *cup-ka'wis,* the barred owl.
Kwaseekho, *kwâ-seek'ho,* the sheldrake.
Lhoks, *locks,* the panther.
Malsun, *măl'sun,* the wolf.
Malsunsis, *măl-sun' sis,* the little wolf cub.
Matwock, *măt'wok,* the white bear.
Meeko, *meek'ō,* the red squirrel.
Megaleep, *meg'â-leep,* the caribou.
Milicete, *mil'ĭ-cete,* the name of an Indian tribe; written also Malicete.
Mitchegeesookh, *mitch-ē-gee'sook,* the snowstorm.
Mitches, *mit'chĕs,* the birch partridge, or ruffed grouse.
Moktaques, *mok-tâ'ques,* the hare.
Mooween, *moo-ween' ,* the black bear.
Mooweesuk, *moo-wee'suk,* the coon.
Musquash, *mus'quâsh,* the muskrat.
Nemox, *nĕm'ox,* the fisher.
Pekompf, *pē-kompf,* the wildcat.
Pekquam, *pek-wăm' ,* the fisher.
Queokh, *quē' ok,* the sea-gull.
Quoskh, *quoskh,* the blue heron.
Seksagadagee, *sek'sâ-gā-dâ'gee,* the Canada grouse, or spruce partridge.
Skooktum, *skook'tum,* the trout.
Tookhees, *tôk'hees,* the wood-mouse.

Umquenawis, *um-que-nâ'wis*, the moose.
Unk Wunk, *unk' wunk*, the porcupine.
Upweekis, *up-week'iss*, the Canada lynx.
Waptonk, *wăp-tonk'*, the wild goose.
Wayeesis, *way-ee'sis*, the white wolf, the strong one.
Whitooweek, *whit-oo-week'*, the woodcock.

Made in United States
Orlando, FL
20 December 2023